The typewriter is holy the poem is holy the voice is
holy the hearers are holy the ecstasy is holy!

—Allen Ginsberg, "Footnote to Howl"

piss factory

16 and time to pay off. I got this job in a piss factory
inspecting pipe. sweating my balls off in this hot like
sahara with no windows xxi real bullshit but its a paycheck
you could faint with the heat but the bitches are too lame
to understand they're getting screwed up the ass too god damn
grateful to get this job them with no teeth gripping gum
or cranium.nothing upstairs the way they suck hot sausage
but then i wasnt saying too much neither.i was moral asshole
hard working school girlgotta earn my doe. no. you gotta
play by the rules find the rythumn within them you got to
relate. floor boss says hey you did your piecework to fast
quit screwing up the quota get off your mustang sa,ly you
aint going nowhere.i swig some romalar and get my nerve up
and put it to hot shit Dot Hook, say hey sister i get bored
it dont matter whether you do labor fast or slow theres always
more after. shes no catholic she says there is ONE REASon
chicken do it my way or i push your face in. we may knee ya
in da john if you dont shape up baby. shake it up baby slow
motion inspection is driving me insane. no windows no diversion
would i could will a radio james brown singing I lost someone
hy lit georgie woods the guy with the goods and guided missles.
nothing here save a porthole in the plaster overlooking sweet
teresa convent. nuns in bloom hoods scatting like eats in
mourning. to me they look pretty damn free out there lucky
not to smooth those hands against hot steel free from the
dogma the in-speed of labor. every afternoon like the last
one like re-run lapping up Dot Hooks midwife sweat some
sound track I prefer the way fags smell and spades and dagos
school boys in heat. the way their legs flap under the desk
in study hall and that forbidden acrid lean amonia smell lilacs
the way they droop like dicks.how long am i condemned to pump
my nostrils full of clammy lady. me i refuse to sweat all i
got under my armpits are a few salt lick hairs peeking like pubes
peeking from my sleeveless I refuse to sweat its 110 degrees
in here i refuse to faint they're all waiting but i aintgonna
faint see the monotany is even more brutal hour after hour
in this piss factory more than ever my fists are assembled I
refuse to lose nothing here to hide save desire hide here save
desire. lucky i lifted rimbauds illuminations from the paper
back forum. it was the face on the cover see rimbauds hair
his sailor face. faire than any boy on the block i was seeing.
my salvation my nosegay the words rocked sex smells coming on
like my brothers sheets before the bath what did i care what
he was saying it was the sound the music the way he was saying
it his words over and over in my skull when I was pumping stel
and she was pumping steel we looked the same but i was getting
my first brain fuck illuminations my salvation oh stolen book
no crime since has been so sweet no perfume ever to fill my nose
no snow no more light then the simple knowledge of you rimbaud
sailor face stolen book hidden inside my blouse so close
to my breast.

Format

low key mac the knife
mac the knife
music fades as I begin introduction
sam
a great human wild animal
devil
the wait for you
christ
working with the pirate
cry me river
white lightning
~~sleepless~~ Fire of unknown origin
jesse james
francois villon
great human wild animal
the murdered boy

Introduction:
this reading is dedicated to all that is criminal
to the great bit of babel
while some built up the tower to the hand of god
others dug deep to stick their tongue in the mouth of hell
to that hell
the rythums of the prison
the great escapes from devils island
the petty thief the whores of mexico
anne powell the only woman Genet could love
the pool halls the hustler
the pirate saint
crimes of passion
the dance of the boxing ring
masters of russian roulette
Johnny Ace
Jackson Pollock james dean
mayakovski
the 38 of the cowboy
gene krupa mary magdeline
the only woman who made our savior weep
and christ himself
christ. greater escape artist then hodini
and the finest faggot in histo ry having 12 men to lick his feet
the radio
the movie camera
blaise cendrars
the electric guitar
and sam shepard

great human wild animal
keep watch over him

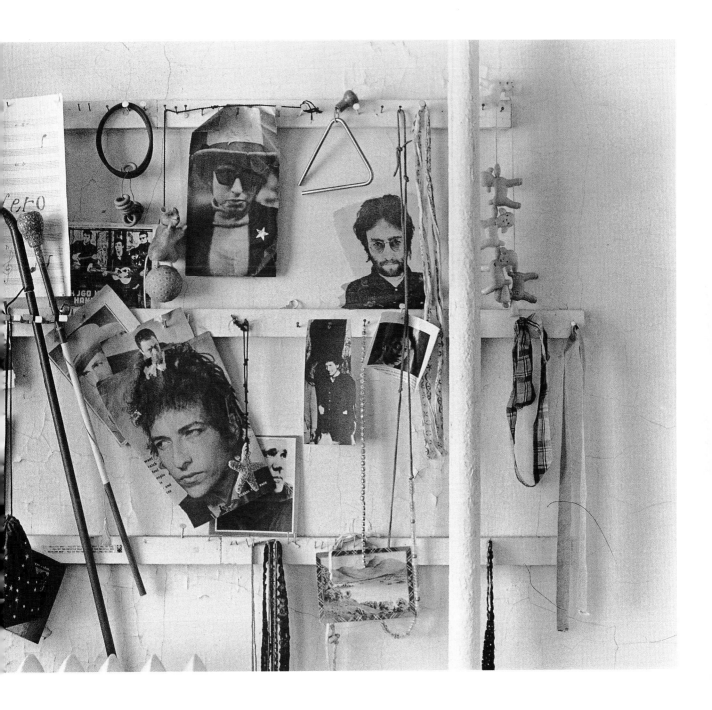

PATTI SMITH

COMPLETE

Lyrics, Reflections & Notes for the Future

DOUBLEDAY

NEW YORK LONDON TORONTO SYDNEY AUCKLAND

FOR TODD

To Find a Voice

The first song I remember singing is "Jesus Loves Me." I can picture myself singing it while sitting on a stoop in Chicago, waiting for the organ grinder to come up the street with his pet monkey. I can hear the songs that were in the air. "Day-O" and "Shrimp Boats" and "Heart of My Hearts." I can hear my father whistling "Deep Purple" and the voice of my mother as she sang us to sleep.

I recall my first record player, only slightly larger than a lunchbox and my two records, one red and one yellow: "Tuby the Tuba" and "Big Rock Candy Mountain." I loved watching them spin, contemplating the worlds they evoked. But the song that made the deepest impression, that produced my first visceral reaction, was sung by Little Richard.

It was Sunday. My mother and I hand in hand. She was taking me to Bible school. She had kid gloves on like the White Rabbit in *Alice in Wonderland*. They gave her a special air and I admired them tremendously. We passed the boys' clubhouse—two huge refrigerator boxes cut and pieced together. Ritchie Glasgow was spinning sides and what wafted from the hand-cut window (more for breathing than for seeing) stopped me dead in my tracks, causing me to let go of my mother's hand so abruptly as to remove her glove.

I didn't know what I was hearing or why I reacted so strongly. It wasn't "Shrimp Boats" or "Day-O." It was something new and though I didn't comprehend what drew me, drawn I was. Drawn into a child's excited dance. That was "Tutti Frutti," so alien, so familiar. That was Little Richard. That was for me the birth of rock and roll.

For a time we lived in Philadelphia. Everyone liked to sing and dance. My sister and I would jitterbug. People sang a cappella on the street corners. When I was nine, we moved to South Jersey. My music teacher adored opera. He would bring his albums to class and play us selections from Verdi and Puccini. I was taken with this music and I was especially moved by Maria Callas. Her emotional intensity. How she seemed to draw from every fiber to create a whisper. Her arias soared from the turntable—especially my favorite, the opera hit single "Un bel di." For a time I dreamed of being an opera singer, but I didn't have the calling, the discipline, or the necessary physical frame. My teacher, sensing my desire, gave me a glorious task. As Manrico I sang the lullaby from Verdi's *Il Trovatore*. For a brief moment I was able to feel the troubadour's expansive love for his home in the mountains.

I dreamed of being a jazz singer like June Christie and Chris Connor. Of approaching songs with the lethargic charge of Billie Holiday. Of championing the downtrodden like Lotte Lenya's "Pirate Jenny." But I never dreamed of singing in a rock and roll band. They had yet to exist in my world. But my world was rapidly changing.

I was privileged to evolve during an inspired period of spiritual and cultural revolution. And the music was the revolution where all had a voice and through this voice we united. Our battlefields were Ohio, Chicago, the Fillmore. We gave new meaning to the word "soldier." We were slinging an electric guitar instead of a machine gun.

I broke from the confines of a rural existence. Farewell the factory, square dance hall, the withering orchards. I headed for New York City. I had in mind to become a painter and through that pursuit I found my beat and the root of my voice. Standing before large sheets of paper tacked to a wall, frustrated with the image I'd draw words instead—rhythms that ran off the page onto the plaster. Writing lyrics evolved from the physical act of drawing words. Later, refining this process led to performance.

In 1969 I moved to the Chelsea Hotel with Robert Mapplethorpe. By then I had abandoned hope of becoming a painter. I was offered work in underground theater. It was too confining. I longed to spar with the people, to make contact. Robert encouraged me to perform my poetry. I attended readings but found them even more confining than theater. Bob Neuwirth suggested I put my lyric style to music and Sam Shepard used two pieces in his play *Mad Dog Blues*.

On February 10, 1971, I gave my first poetry reading, opening for Gerard Malanga at St. Mark's Church on the Bowery. In desiring to project a raw energy, I recruited Lenny Kaye. We climaxed the reading with his sonic interpretation of a stock car race with electric guitar while I read "Ballad of a Bad Boy." It seemed to have a negative effect. I took that as a positive sign.

In the next few years I took to studying Hank Williams, got me a Bob Dylan songbook, banged away on an old thirties Gibson. I worked in a bookstore. I drew. I modeled for Robert. Scrawled in my notebooks. I wandered through the debris of the sixties. So much joy yet malcontent. So many voices raised, then snuffed. My generation's heritage seemed to be in jeopardy.

These things were on my mind: the course of the artist, the course of freedom redefined, the re-creation of space, the emergence of new voices.

And these things I came to express—albeit somewhat awkwardly—through the form of rock and roll. Perhaps I have been none but a scrappy pawn, but I am nonetheless grateful for the moves I came to make.

And salute all who helped me make them.

vera gemini

Oh your the kind of girl
Id like to find in my mirror
you have all the markings
of the devil girl
yet you are boned like a saint
with the conscience of a snake

Oh your eyes have shifted from me
everyone saw what you did
how you slipped from beneath me.
live a nervous squid
a little false and frigid
the whole crowd knew you did it

yes you have behaved treacherously
and in public too my vera marie
so i believe you'll have to pay

i said you be good or go to hell
in my arms ill be happy to sail you there
my lovely

Oh no more horses horses
were gonna swim like fish
into the hole in which
you planned to ditch me

you have filled me with a vengence
and touched me with your breath
and planned to leave me cold
but you'll never get your wish
im gonna pull you from the dance
you writhe you ride so easily
im gonna gather up your reins in my fist
just me and you
one two
oh no more horses
horses horses

I was your victom
I was well decieved
hells built on regrets
and i hold to many
i love your naked neck
even the lies youve told me
a lily thats bend lying
white and bent and sick

Oh but you arent two faced
you have two faces
that will speak no more no more no more

Oh your the knid of girl
i found in my mirror
laughing
the way you laughed at christ
oh he fell on frid y
rose on monday
but when i take you down you wont rise

Horses

All the wisdom of the universe can be found between the eyes of the horse.

— Qur'an

The Joker Is Wild

The pursuit of style has always been a spirited part of the work process. Images that inform the work or the movement of the work. Baudelaire's cravat. June Christie's careless ponytail. A raincoat à la Camus. Bob Dylan's snap tab collar. Black capris like Ava Gardner. Discarded finery from rich heaps. Italian sunglasses. Green silk stockings. Ballet slippers. Boxer shoes. A sense of style. A certain body language. A simple, intricate gesture. More often than not, bred from innocence, awkwardness, or pure survival.

I overslept the day we shot the cover of *Horses*. I dressed hastily in the clothes I wore, like a uniform, on the stage and in the street. Robert worked swiftly, wordlessly. He had a nervous, confident manner. He had no assistant. There was a triangle of shadow he wanted. The light was changing. The triangle fading. He asked me to remove my jacket because he liked the white of my shirt. I tossed the jacket over my shoulder Sinatra-style, hopefully capturing some of his casual defiance. That was the shot Robert chose.

When I look at it now, I believe we captured some of the anthemic artlessness of our age. Of our generation. A breed apart who sought within a new landscape to excite, to astonish, and to resonate with all the possibilities of our youth.

By 1974, Lenny Kaye and I had teamed up with Richard Sohl, a gifted, intuitive piano player—part Motown, part Mendelssohn. We developed our style, a heightened form of communication within a three-chord field. We released an independent single, "Hey Joe/Piss Factory," and through the efforts of Jane Friedman and the Wartoke Concern I was signed by Clive Davis for Arista Records. As we developed, we brought Ivan Kral and Jay Dee Daugherty into the fold and formed the Patti Smith Group.

"Gloria" was bred of this time, crossing the poem "Oath," written in 1970, with the Van Morrison classic. It was to be the first PSG single and in the words of writer Paul Williams, "a declaration of existence." "Gloria" gave me the opportunity to acknowledge and disclaim our musical and spiritual heritage. It personifies for me, within its adolescent conceit, what I hold sacred as an artist. The right to create, without apology, from a stance beyond gender or social definition, but not beyond the responsibility to create something of worth.

Gloria (In Excelsis Deo)

Jesus died for somebody's sins but not mine
Melting in a pot of thieves wild card up my sleeve
Thick heart of stone my sins my own
They belong to me. Me

People say beware but I don't care
The words are just rules and regulations to me. Me
I walk in a room you know I look so proud
I move in this here atmosphere where anything's allowed
And I go to this here party but I just get bored
Until I look out the window see a sweet young thing
Humping on the parking meter leaning on the parking meter
Oh, she looks so good. Oh, she looks so fine
And I got this crazy feeling that I'm gonna make her mine

Put my spell on her here she comes
Walking down the street here she comes
Coming through my door here she comes
Crawling up my stair here she comes
Waltzing through the hall in a pretty red dress
And oh, she looks so good. Oh, she looks so fine
And I got this crazy feeling that I'm gonna make her mine

Then I hear this knocking on my door hear this knocking on my door
And I look up at the big tower clock and say oh my God it's midnight
And my baby is walking through the door leaning on my couch
And she whispers to me and I take the big plunge
And oh, she was so good. And oh, she was so fine
And I'm gonna tell the world that I just made her mine

And I said darling tell me your name. She told me her name
She whispered to me she told me her name and her name is
And her name is and her name is and her name is G-L-O-R-I-A

G-L-O-R-I-A Gloria G-L-O-R-I-A Gloria
G-L-O-R-I-A Gloria G-L-O-R-I-A Gloria

It was at the stadium. There were twenty thousand girls
Called their names out to me Marie Ruth but to tell you the truth
I didn't hear them. I didn't see. I let my eyes rise to the big tower clock
And I heard those bells chiming in my heart going ding-dong
Ding-dong ding-dong ding-dong ding-dong ding-dong ding-dong
Ding-dong. Calling the time when you came to my room
And you whispered to me and we took the big plunge
And oh, you were so good. Oh, you were so fine
And I've got to tell the world that I made her mine made her mine
Made her mine made her mine made her mine made her mine

G-L-O-R-I-A Gloria
G-L-O-R-I-A Gloria
G-L-O-R-I-A Gloria

And the tower bells chime
ding-dong
They chime
I said

Jesus died for somebody's sins
but not mine

the women were singing
of a girl who was snatched

...veins full of existance—
sad description / but oh I was
listening for
.... like the son of a rock Relice   you

Shape of a young man dressed in a coat of
milk.

Redondo Beach
it was late afternoon
dreaming
Hotel
we had just had the quarrel
that sent you away
I was looking for you—oh
and you were gone gone
called you on the phone
Johnny no answer
she never returned
oh you know what I mean
I was etc.

down by the

women
sad description / but oh I was looking
for you—

The desk clerk told

she

THE words for "Redondo Beach" were written in 1971. I was sharing a space near the Chelsea Hotel with Robert and my sister Linda. One afternoon I had a rare argument with my sister and she left. She didn't return and by nightfall I was worried. Needing time to think, I took an F train to Coney Island and sat on the littered beach until the sun rose. I came back, wrote the draft and fell asleep. When I awoke, she had returned. I showed her what I had written and we never quarreled again.

Redondo Beach

Late afternoon dreaming hotel
We just had the quarrel that sent you away
I was looking for you are you gone gone
Call you on the phone another dimension
Well you never returned oh you know what I mean
I went looking for you are you gone gone
Down by the ocean it was so dismal
Women all standing with shock on their faces
Sad description oh I was looking for you

Everyone was singing girl is washed up
On Redondo Beach and everyone is so sad
I was looking for you are you gone gone

Pretty little girl everyone cried
She was the victim of sweet suicide
I went looking for you are you gone gone

Down by the ocean it was so dismal
Women all standing with shock on their faces
Sad description oh I was looking for you

Desk clerk told me girl was washed up
Was small and angel with apple blonde hair now
I went looking for you are you gone gone

Picked up my key didn't reply
Went to my room started to cry
You were small and angel are you gone gone

Down by the ocean it was so dismal
I was just standing with shock on my face
The hearse pulled away and the girl that had died it was you
You'll never return into my arms cause you are gone gone
Never return into my arms cause you are gone gone
Gone gone gone gone
Good-bye

Shaman Doo-Wop

The concept of improvisation has long repelled and excited me, for it contains the possibilities of humiliation and illumination. Like Beethoven, John Coltrane elevated improvisation as a spiritual course. Going out and coming back. Offering up a melodic theme, going off to talk to God, then returning to talk to us.

Johnny Carson inspired another sense of spiel. The master of monologue, he could move out and deliver off the cuff. He was the human parachute, able to bail out of any situation with the perfect comeback. Just like John Barrymore.

I first experienced improvising before a live audience in 1971, writing and performing the play *Cowboy Mouth* with Sam Shepard. Our characters, Slim and Cavale, would spar in a poetic language drawn from the air, the energy of the people, and our own devices. Sam offered simple counsel: "If you miss a beat, make up another."

Perhaps I had a knack for this. Coupled by studying my favorite Johnnys. I liked the immediacy, the transmutation of energy. I liked the task of drawing from oneself. One's ancestors. One's God. To be a human saxophone.

"Birdland" is an example of how a lyric is composed live in the studio. It is the result of the trust built between musicians, requiring communal selflessness in order to draw from the collective intelligence. One tells the tale in the process. "Birdland" originated as a piece called "The Harbor Song," a metaphoric voyage of birds in underwater flight. Richard and I, propelled by Lenny, would take it to the edge, then return. I can still picture Richard, his eyes like saucers, following, then staying in step, anticipating my next move.

The "Birdland" documented here was inspired by a passage from Peter Reich's *Book of Dreams*. His father Wilhelm Reich had died, and during a family gathering he thought he saw the lights of a spaceship while the song "Party Doll" was blaring. He believed his father to be at the helm. But despite his desperate cries, the light vanished into the night sky as Peter lay on the grass, weeping beneath the stars.

Birdland

His father died and left him a little farm in New England.
All the long black funeral cars left the scene.
And the boy was just standing there alone,
Looking at the shiny red tractor
Him and his daddy used to sit inside
And circle the blue fields and grease the night.
It was as if someone had spread butter on all the fine points of the stars
'Cause when he looked up they started to slip.
Then he put his head in the crux of his arm
And he started to drift, drift to the belly of a ship,
Let the ship slide open, and he went inside of it,
And saw his daddy behind the control board streaming beads of light.
He saw his daddy behind the control board,
And he was very different tonight
'Cause he was not human, he was not human.
The little boy's face lit up with such naked joy
That the sun burned around his lids and his eyes were like two suns,
White lids, white opals, seeing everything just a little bit too clearly
And he looked around and there was no black ship in sight,
No black funeral cars, nothing except for him the raven
And he fell on his knees and looked up and cried out,
No, daddy, don't leave me here alone,
Take me up, daddy, to the belly of your ship,
Let the ship slide open and I'll go inside of it
Where you're not human, you are not human.

But nobody heard the boy's cry of alarm.
Nobody there except for the birds around the New England farm
And they gathered in all directions, like roses they scattered,
And they were like compass grass coming together into the head of a
Shaman bouquet. Slit in his nose and all the others went shooting
And he saw the lights of traffic beckoning like the hands of Blake
Grabbing at his cheeks, taking out his neck, all his limbs,
Everything was twisted and he said:
I won't give up, won't give up, don't let me give up,
I won't give up, come here, let me go up fast,
Take me up quick, take me up, up to the belly of a ship
And the ship slides open and I go inside of it
Where I am not human.

I am helium raven and this movie is mine,
So he cried out as he stretched the sky,
Pushing it all out like latex cartoon,
Am I all alone in this generation?
We'll just be dreaming of animation night and day
And it won't let up, won't let up and I see them coming in,
Oh, I couldn't hear them before, but I hear them now,
It's a radar scope in all silver and all platinum lights
Moving in like black ships, they were moving in, streams of them,
And he put up his hands and he said:
It's me, it's me, I'll give you my eyes, take me up,
Oh now please take me up, I'm helium raven
Waiting for you, please take me up, don't leave me here.

The son, the sign, the cross, like the shape of a tortured woman,
The true shape of a tortured woman, the mother standing
In the doorway letting her sons, no longer presidents but prophets.
They're all dreaming they're going to bear the prophet,
He's going to run through the fields dreaming in animation
It's all going to split his skull, it's going to come out
Like a black bouquet shining, like a fist that's going to shoot them up
Like light, like Mohammed Boxer, take them up up up up up up.
Oh, let's go up up take me up I'll go up I'm going up I'm going up.
Take me up, I'm going up, I'll go up there.
Go up go up go up go up up up up up up
Up, up to the belly of a ship. Let the ship slide open.
We'll go inside of it where we are not human, we are not human.

Where there was sand, there were tiles,
The sun had melted the sand and it coagulated like a river of glass
When it hardened he looked at the surface, he saw his face
And where there were eyes were just two white opals, two white opals,
Where there were eyes there were just two white opals,
And he looked up, and the rays shot, and he saw raven coming in,
And he crawled on his back and he went up up up up up up up.
Sha da do wop da shaman do way sha da do wop da shaman do way
Sha da do wop da shaman do way sha da do wop da shaman do way

We like birdland.

Free Money

Every night before I go to sleep
Find a ticket win a lottery
Scoop the pearls up from the sea
Cash them in and buy you all the things you need

Every night before I rest my head
See those dollar bills go swirling round my bed
I know they're stolen but I don't feel bad
I take that money buy you things you never had

Oh baby it would mean so much to me
Oh baby to buy you all the things you need for free
I'll buy you a jet plane baby
Get you on a higher plane to a jet stream
And take you through the stratosphere
And check out the planets there and then take you down
Deep where it's hot hot in Arabia-babia
Then cool cold fields of snow. And we'll roll
Dream roll dream roll dream roll dream

When we dream it when we dream it when we dream it
We'll dream it dream it for free free money free money free
Money free money free money free money free money

Every night before I go to sleep
Find a ticket win a lottery
Every night before I rest my head
See those dollar bills go swirling round my bed

Oh baby it would mean so much to me
Baby I know our troubles will be gone
Oh I know our troubles will be gone going gone
If we dream dream dream for free

And when we dream it when we dream it when we dream it
Let's dream it we'll dream it for free free money free money
Free money free money free money free money free money

In the field, about a hundred feet from the black barn, was the great bush-tree. It was alive and vibrating, all the words of God. I spent long hours praying to it. When I was twelve my sister was born. One afternoon the sky went pitch. A storm was coming. I was holding Kimberly in my arms. The air was like milk. I was fed up with prayers. I was fed up with everything. I stared at the bush for a long time. I wanted something. I cradled the baby's skull. It was a lightbulb. I concentrated as hard as I could. Lightning struck. Her face lit up. Everything in flames. The world was turning all the destructive whims of nature. Rivers drying, rivers of salt remaining, berserk waterfowl kamikazing into raging falls. The barn was crumbling. The bush was burning. And Kimberly was shining in my hands like a phosphorescent living doll.

notes, august 2, 1975

20

Kimberly

The wall is high the black barn
The babe in my arms in her swaddling clothes
And I know soon that the sky will split
And the planets will shift
Balls of jade will drop and existence will stop

Little sister the sky is falling
I don't mind I don't mind
Little sister the fates are calling on you

Here I stand again in this old electric whirlwind
The sea rushes up my knees like flame
And I feel like just some misplaced Joan of Arc
And the cause is you looking up at me
Oh baby I remember when you were born
It was dawn and the storm settled in my belly
And I rolled in the grass and I spit out the gas
And I lit a match and the void went flash
And the sky split and the planets hit
Balls of jade dropped and existence stopped

Little sister the sky is falling
I don't mind I don't mind
Little sister the fates are calling on you

I was young and crazy so crazy I knew
I could break through with you
So with one hand I rocked you
And with one heart I reached for you
Ah I knew your youth was for the taking
Fire on a mental plane so I ran through the fields
As the bats with their baby vein faces
Burst from the barn in flames into the violent violet sky
And I fell on my knees and pressed you against me
Your skull was like a network of spittle
Like glass balls moving in like cold streams of logic
And I prayed as the lightning attacked
That something would make it go crack

Something will make it go crack
Something will make it go crack
Something will make it go crack

The palm trees fall into the sea
It doesn't matter much to me
As long as you're safe Kimberly
And I can gaze deep into your starry eyes
Looking deep in your eyes baby
Looking deep in your eyes baby
Looking deep in your eyes baby
Into your starry eyes

Fire of Unknown Origin

A fire of unknown origin took my baby away
Fire of unknown origin took my baby away
Swept her up and off my wavelength
Swallowed her up like the ocean in a fire thick and gray
Death comes sweeping through the hallway like a lady's dress
Death comes riding down the highway in its Sunday best
Death comes riding death comes creeping
Death comes I can't do nothing
Death goes there must be something that remains
Death it made me sick and crazy
Cause that fire it took my baby away

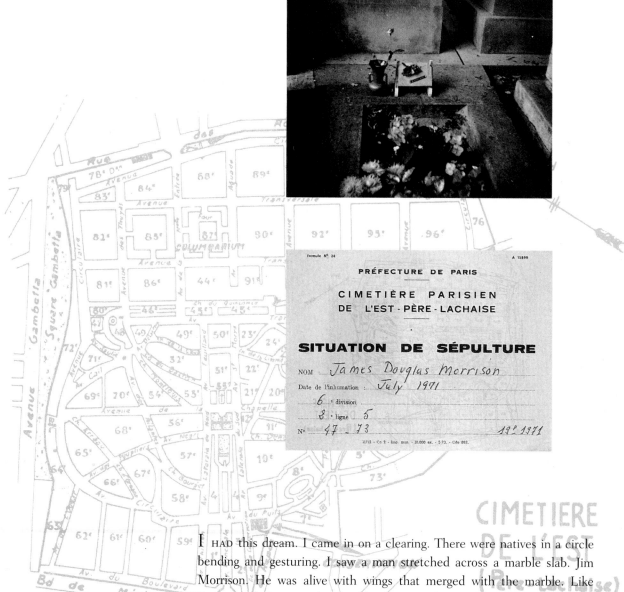

I HAD this dream. I came in on a clearing. There were natives in a circle bending and gesturing. I saw a man stretched across a marble slab. Jim Morrison. He was alive with wings that merged with the marble. Like Prometheus, he struggled, but freedom was beyond him. I stood over him chanting, break it up break it up break it up break it up. Code etched like some new hieroglyphics. Break it up Jim break it up Jim break it up. Hours like orders, passing like water. Break it up Jim break it up Jim break it up. Time moved as my mouth. The stone dissolved and he moved away. I brushed the feathers from my hair, adjusted my pillow and returned to sleep. Tom Verlaine and I composed these words.

notes, december 1974

Break It Up

Car stopped in a clearing
Ribbon of life, it was nearing
I saw the boy break out of his skin
My heart turned over and I crawled in
He cried break it up, oh, I don't understand
Break it up, I can't comprehend
Break it up, oh, I want to feel you
Break it up, don't talk to me that way
I'm not listening

Snow started falling
I could hear the angel calling
We rolled on the ground, he stretched out his wings
The boy flew away and he started to sing
He sang break it up, oh, I don't understand
Break it up, I can't comprehend
Break it up, oh, I want to feel you
Break it up, don't look at me
The sky was raging. The boy disappeared
I fell on my knees. Atmosphere broke up
The boy reappeared. I cried take me please

Ice it was shining. I could feel my heart it was melting
I tore off my clothes, I danced on my shoes
I ripped my skin open and then I broke through, I cried
Break it up, oh, now I understand
Break it up, and I want to go
Break it up, oh, please take me with you
Break it up, I can feel it breaking
I can feel it breaking, I can feel it breaking
I can feel, I can feel, I can feel, I can feel
So break it up, oh, now I'm coming with you
Break it up now I'm going to go
Break it up oh feel me I'm coming
Break it up break it up break it up
Break it up break it up break it up
Break it up break it up break it up

who pulls the strings. I'd like to know
who is the man who serves as the model.
who made woman the loser. who claimed
birth right. who gave my mama the right
to bear me. who can understand the
symphony in my head. the festival. the
war. the radium mind.who can hear what
I'm thinking as I'm thinking. why is
my left eye walleyed. why am i up
against a wall now. how can desire
remain desire. do i have a tapeworm
do i have bad blood

THE photographer Kate Simon shot William Burroughs and I in his
quarters on Franklin Street on my twenty-ninth birthday. We had released *Horses* and I owed no small debt to him, for the hero of "Land"
was truly a descendant of his Johnny in *The Wild Boys*. William was
highly supportive and it was an honor to see him sitting at a table close
to the stage when we played CBGBs.

It was an amplified period of exploration with poets Tom Verlaine and Richard Hell at the forefront. Needing our own niche, they found an untapped derelict bar on the Bowery. The proprietor, Hilly Crystal, allowed a small stage to be built and CBGB became ours. Together with bands like Television, we sought, we shattered, we excited ourselves. There were no rules, no sudden material expectations. William generously gave us a nod, often smiling at the notion that he was the spiritual father of another generation of Johnnys.

Land

Horses

The boy was in the hallway drinking a glass of tea
From the other end of the hallway a rhythm was generating
Another boy was sliding up the hallway
He merged perfectly with the hallway
He merged perfectly the mirror in the hallway
The boy looked at Johnny Johnny wanted to run
but the movie kept moving as planned
The boy took Johnny he pressed him against the locker
He drove it in he drove it home he drove it deep in Johnny
The boy disappeared Johnny fell on his knees
started crashing his head against the locker
started crashing his head against the locker
started laughing hysterically
When suddenly Johnny
gets the feeling
he's being surrounded by
horses horses horses horses
coming in all directions
white shining silver studs with their nose in flames
He saw horses horses horses
horses horses horses horses horses

Land of a Thousand Dances

Do you know how to pony like bony maroney
Do you know how to twist well it goes like this it goes like this
Then you mash potato do the alligator do the alligator
And you twista twista like your baby sister
I want your baby sister give me your baby sister teach your baby sister
To rise up from her knees do the sweet pea do the sweet pee pee
Roll down on her back got to lose control got to lose control
Got to lose control and then you take control
Then you roll down on your back
Do you like it like that like it like that
Then you do the watusi yeah do the watusi
Life is filled with holes Johnny's laying there in his sperm coffin
Angel looks down at him and says ah pretty boy
Can't you show me nothing but surrender
Johnny gets up takes off his leather jacket
Taped to his chest there's the answer
He got pen knives and jack knives and
Switchblades preferred switchblades preferred
He cries he screams says
Life is full of pain I push it through my brain
And I fill my nose with snow and go Rimbaud
Go Rimbaud go Rimbaud go Johnny go
And do the watusi oh do the watusi

There's a little place a place called space
It's a pretty little place it's across the track
Across the track and the name of that place
Is I like it like that I like it like that
I like it like that I like it like that
And the name of the band is the Twistelettes
Twistelette twistelette twistelette
Twistelette twistelette twistelette

La Mer (de)

Let it calm down let it calm down
In the night in the eye of the forest
There's a mare black and shining with yellow hair
I put my fingers through her silken hair
And found a stair I didn't waste time
I just walked right up and saw that up there
There is a sea up there there is a sea up there
There is a sea seize the possibility
There is no land but the land
[Up there is just a sea of possibilities]
There is no sea but the sea
[Up there is a wall of possibilities]
There is no keeper but the key
[Up there there are several walls of possibilities]
Except for one who seizes possibilities
I seize the first possibility the sea around me
I was standing there with my legs spread like a sailor
[in a sea of possibilities] I felt his hand on my knee

[On the screen] And I looked at Johnny
And handed him a branch of coral flame
[In the heart of man] The waves were coming in
Like Arabian stallions gradually lapping into sea horses
He picked up the blade and he pressed it against
His smooth throat and let it dip in [the veins]
Dip in to the sea the sea of possibilities
It started hardening it started hardening in my hand
And I felt the arrows of desire

I put my hand inside his cranium, oh we had such a brainiac-amour
But no more, no more I gotta move from my mind to the area
[Go Rimbaud go Rimbaud go Rimbaud] Oh go Johnny go
Do the watusi, yeah do the watusi do the watusi
His skull shot open coiled snakes white and shiny twirling and encircling
Our lives are now entwined we will four years be together twining
Your nerves the mane of the black shining horse
And my fingers all entwined through your silky hair
I could feel it it was the hair going through my fingers
[Build it build it]

The hairs were like wires going through my body
I that's how I that's how I died
Oh that Tower of Babel they knew what they were after
They knew what they were after
Everything on the current moved up
I tried to stop it but it was too warm
[No possible ending, no possible ending]
Too unbelievably smooth like playing in the sea
In the sea of possibility the possibility was a blade
A shiny blade I hold the key to the sea of possibilities
There's no land but the land looked at my hands
And there's a red stream that went streaming through
The sands like fingers like arteries like fingers
[All wisdom fixed between the eyes of a horse]
He lay pressing it against his throat [your eyes]
He opened his throat [your eyes] his vocal chords
Started shooting like [of a horse] mad pituitary glands
The scream he made [my heart] was so high
[My heart] pitched that nobody heard no one heard
That cry no one heard [Johnny] the butterfly flapping
In his throat his fingers nobody heard he was on that bed
It was like a sea of jelly and so he seized the first
His vocal chords shot up [possibility] like mad pituitary glands
It was a black tube he felt himself disintegrate
[There is nothing happening at all] and go inside the black tube
So when he looked out into the street
Saw this sweet young thing
Humping on the parking meter
Leaning on the parking meter
In the sheets there was a man
Everything around him unraveling like some long Fender whine
Dancing around to the simple rock and roll song

Elegie

I just don't know what to do tonight
My head is aching as I drink and breathe
Memory falls like cream in my bones
Moving on my own
There must be something I can dream tonight
The air is filled with the moves of you
All the fire is frozen yet still I have the will
Trumpets, violins, I hear them in the distance
And my skin emits a ray
But I think it's sad, it's much too bad
That our friends can't be with us today

Radio Ethiopia

Beauty will be convulsive or not at all.

—André Breton, *Nadja*

Reprinted courtesy of The Yipster Times *(March-April, 1977). A subscription to* The Yipster Times *is only $6/yr. to P.O. Box 392, Canal Street Station, New York, NY 10013. The Patti Smith Group's new record is* Radio Ethiopia *on Arista Records. Patti says:* "Radio Ethiopia *goes beyond the wax into a disc of light. Fight the good fight."*

You Can't Say "Fuck" in Radio Free America

BY PATTI SMITH

New Year's Eve, Patti Smith gave a concert at NYC's Palladium. WNEW-FM refused to air the concert on their station due to her using the word "fuck" on an interview with the station last November. Upon hearing of this decision, Patti wrote this heavy condemnation of "progressive' rock radio as we hear it now.

Fuck the word...fuck the word
fuck the word the word is dead
is re-defined...the bird in the (womb)
is expelled by the propelling
motion of fuck of fucking

On November 29, Patti Smith delivered an address on WNEW-FM in New York City. Because of the content of this message, the Patti Smith Group will not be aired live in the future on Metromedia. A transcript is available to the people, for the people who support free communication to decide what programming they want to hear on their radio. (S.s.a.e. to Radio Ethiopia, P.O. Box 188, Mantua, New Jersey 08051).

THE RESISTANCE

We believe in the total freedom of communication and we will not be compromised. The censorship of words is as meaningless as the censorship of musical notes; we cannot tolerate either. Freedom means exactly that: no limits, no boundaries...rock and roll is not a colonial power to be exploited, told what to say and how to say it. This is the spirit in which our music began and the flame in which it must be continued. Radio Ethiopia is a symphony of experience...each piece a movement...14 movements...14 stations.

There is silence on my radio...
-Stones

They are trying to silence us, but they cannot succeed. We cannot be "trusted" not to pollute the airwaves with our idealism and intensity. W(New) York radio has proved unresponsive at best to the new rock and roll being born under its ears...a music having worldwide cause and effect...injecting a new sense of urgency and imperative. Radio has consistently lagged behind the needs of the community it is honor-bound to serve. We do not consider paternalistic token airplay and passive coverage to be enough. FM radio was birthed in the 1960's as an alternative to

restrictive playlisting and narrow monopolistic visions. The promise is being betrayed.

We Want The Radio And We Want It Now 1977...the celebration of 1776-1976 ends tonight... we end with the same desires of individual and ethnic freedom of concept...the freedom of art...the freedom of work...the freedom/flow of energy that keeps re-building itself with the nourishment of each generation. The political awareness of the 1960's was a result of the political repression of the 1950's. The 70's have rep-resented the merging of both...political-artistic/activism-expression.

The colonial year is dead. Rock and roll is not a colonial art. We colonize to further the freedom of space.

We must dedicate ourselves to the future...in the sixties the DOG was GOD...the underdogs rose up and merged and fought for political freedom... we of 1977 are Rat/Art.

---Radio Ethiopia, 1977

suspended in relics (art)...The guardians of ritual salute all that heralds and redefines civilization into a long streaming system of tongues...salute then spit on those who left us the ruins of much broken ground then move on...

dedicated to the future we are thus fasting...we rip into the past/perfect like raw meat...we do not accept the past as the summit of creation...we rise and pierce the membrane of mire and waste...the stagnation of rust...

1977. We the people of the neo-army are spewing JUST LUST...The absolute motion into the future... To fight the good fight...the fight for feedom of ex-pression...The fight against fat and Roman satisfaction.

WE DON'T WANT NO SATISFACTION
!!THE ART/RAT DAWNS!!
(THE AWAKENING GRAIN)

RAISE UP/ TAKE POSITION/ DUO-SONIC THE SYSTEM OF GOD. ILLUMINATED WEAPONS POISED LIKE MALLOTS LIKE 2-SOUND PICK-UPS BAYONETING THE FLESH OF THE EYE...A GRAIN OF SAND THRU THE OPTIC NERVES OF HE THAT SEIZE ALL...A·ʀ (rasive) AND STONED AND IR-RATED BY A SPECT(RÉ) SO CUNNING HE EVEN-TUALLY SHOWS HIS PHASE HE EVENTUALLY WAKES UP) (SHARP AND ROUGH AND DELICATE-LY CUT THE AWAKENING GRAIN DOES ITS WORK! THE ART/RAT DAWNS AGAIN! ART/RAT KNAWS THRU SPACE/ RUSHING TADPOLES/ A BLACK STREAK ACROSS THE WHITE HOTEL... THE GLASS THAT SEPARATES HIM FROM SOCIETY IS THE TRUE PRISON OF LIGHT...ART/ RAT IN THE SHAPE OF A BOY DRESSED IN A COAT OF MILK...ACTION PAINTER...RUBEDO HAIR OF THE ONE WHO SOARS AND SLASHES THRU THE AVIATOR BACK/FLAP W/OUT BAR-ING THE SENCE OF PURE TONGUE RYTHUM... ART/RAT POSSESING THE NOBEL CONCEIT OF THE FUTURE AWAITS HIGH ORDERS TO SPEW THE TONGUE OF LOVE THAT UTTERS THE MOST PRECIOUS COMMAND THE WORDS OF LOVE THAT TURN US ON (THE PHYSICAL HIEROGLYPHICS))(THE 14 POSITIONS) ARE "FUCK ME FUCK ME FUCK ME FUCK ME...FUCK THE WORD/ THE WORD IS DEAD/ FUCK IS DEAD ON THE RADIO/ THE WORD IS DEAD/ IN A WAVE OF SOUND/ TO BE UNBOUND AND WAVED AND DEFILED LIKE A BANNER OUTSIDE SOCIETY OVER THE BLACK RIVER...CITIZENS ARISE! SPIT–BALL INTO "THE SKY! THE AWAKENING GRAIN AWAKENING A–WAKE UP W

PERHAPS it was the repetition of performing, for the flow of language that seemed infinite, that poured through my hand onto sheets of paper onto the wall and into the air, seemed to dry up as we created *Radio Ethiopia*. How then to communicate? To reinvent words. Disassociate them. Redefine them. Fuck the slang scrawled across our practice room walls.

I went up to 48th Street and got me an electric guitar. A 1957 Fender Duo-Sonic. Old Mr. Manny sold it to me, on time, for $110. Legend had it that Jimi Hendrix had played it. Legend or not, it was mine. The thick maple neck, strung with god's heaviest strings, felt good to me. I wasn't interested in learning chords, I was interested in expressing ideas, however abstract, within the realm of sound.

It was the bicentennial year. The force of desire compelled us to translate imagination into action. It was at this time while attempting to mount a tide of feedback that I met Fred Sonic Smith, who with few words showed me the way to draw from my instrument another language, or as he put it, to be sonically speaking.

— notes, new york city, 1976

Ask the Angels

Move. Ask the angels who they're calling
Go ask the angels if they're calling to thee
Ask the angels while they're falling
Who that person could possibly be
And I know you got the feeling
You know I feel it crawling across the floor
And I know it got you reeling
And honey honey the call is for war
And it's wild wild wild wild

Everybody got the feeling
You know the feeling
And it's stronger each day
Everybody wants to be reeling
And baby baby I'll show you the way
Across the country through the fields
You know I see it written across the sky
People rising from the highway
And war war is the battle cry
And it's wild wild wild wild

Armageddon it's gotten
No savior jailer can take it from me
World ending it's just beginning
And rock n roll is what I'm born to be
And it's wild wild wild wild
Wild wild wild wild
Wild wild wild wild
Ask the angels if they're starting to move
Coming in droves in from L.A.
Ask the angels if they're starting to groove
Light as our armor and it's today
It's wild wild wild wild
Wild wild wild wild
Wild wild wild wild

Ain't It Strange

Down in Vineland there's a clubhouse
Girl in white dress boy shoot white stuff
Oh don't you know that anyone can join
And they come and they call and they fall on the floor
Don't you see when you're looking at me
That I'll never end transcend transcend
Ain't it strange oh oh oh
Ain't it strange oh oh oh
Come and join me I implore thee
I implore thee come explore me
Oh don't you know that anyone can come
And they come and they call and they crawl on the floor
Don't you see when you're looking at me
That I'll never end transcend transcend
Ain't it strange oh oh oh
Ain't it strange oh oh oh
True true who are you
Who who am I

Down in Vineland there's a clubhouse
Girl in white dress boy shoot white stuff
Oh don't you know that anyone can come
And they come and they call and they fall on the floor
Don't you see when you're looking at me
That I'll never end transcend transcend
Ain't it strange oh oh oh
Ain't it strange oh oh oh

do you go to the temple tonight oh no i don't think so do you not go to the
palace of answers with me marie oh no i don't think so no see when they offer
me book of gold i know soon still that platinum is coming and when I look
inside of your temple it looks just like the inside of any one man and when he
beckons his finger to me well i move in another direction i move in another
dimension i move in another dimension oh oh oh

Hand of God I feel the finger
Hand of God I start to whirl
Hand of God I do not linger

Don't get dizzy do not fall now
Turn whirl like a dervish
Turn God make a move
Turn Lord
I don't get nervous
I just move in another dimension
Come move in another dimension
Come move in another dimension
Come move in another dimension
Strange strange

do you go to the temple tonight oh no i don't think so no will you go to the
pagoda the palace of answers with me marie oh no i don't believe so no see
when they offer me book of gold i know soon still that platinum is coming
and when i look inside of your temple it looks just like the inside of any one
man and when he beckons his finger to me well i move in another dimension
i move in another dimension i move in another dimension

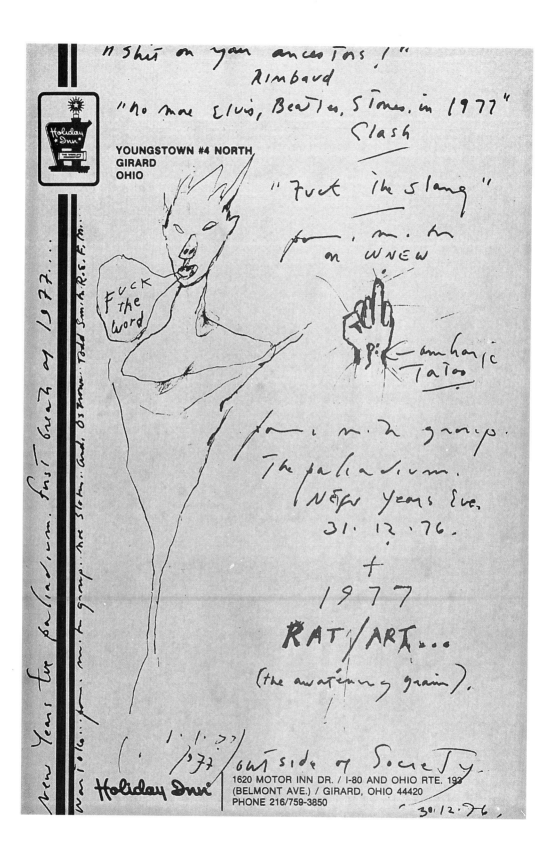

FIELD MARSHALL

Poppies

Heard it on the radio it's no good
Heard it on the radio it's news to me
When she getting something it's understood
Baby's got something she's not used to
Down down poppy yeah
Waiting on the corner wanna score
Baby wants something she's in the mood to
Baby wants something I want more
When I don't get it I get blue blue
Down down and it's really coming
Really coming down down poppy yeah

She was tense and gleaming in the sun
They split her open like a country
Everyone was very pleased to be a state of
Her mind was gently probed like a finger
Everything soaking and spread with butter
And then they laid her on the table
She connected with the inhaler
And the needle was shifting like crazy
She was she was completely still
It was like a painting of a vase
She just lay there and the gas traveled fast
Thru the dorsal spine and down and around
The anal cavity her cranium it was really great man
The gas had inflicted her entire spine
With the elements of a voluptuous disease
With a green vapor made her feet light
I moved thru the door I saw the wheel and it was golden
And oh my God I finally scored
I turned the channel station after station
I don't think there's any station
Quite as interesting to me as the 12th station
I tuned in to the tower too many centuries
Were calling to me spinning down thru time

Oh watch them say you're too high
Before him we didn't worship suffering
Didn't we laugh and dance for hours
 We were having fun as we built the tower
I saw it spiraling up into his electric eye
I felt it go in and started to cry
Oh God are you afraid
Why did the tower turn you off babe
I want to feel you in my radio
Goddamn in my radio
If you want to go go if you want to see
If you want to go as far as she
You must look God in the face
Heard it on the radio heard it on the radio
One long ecstatic pure sensation restriction started excreting
Started excreting ah exhilarating bottomless pit
Hey Sheba hey Salome hey Venus eclipsing my way ah
You're vessel every woman is a vessel is evasive is aquatic
Everyone silver ecstatic platinum disk spinning

Pissing in a River

Pissing in a river watching it rise
Tattoo fingers shy away from me
Voices voices mesmerize
Voices voices beckoning sea
Come come come come back come back
Come back come back come back
Spoke of a wheel tip of a spoon
Mouth of a cave I'm a slave I'm free
When are you coming hope you come soon
Fingers fingers encircling thee
Come come come come come come
Come come come come come come for me
My bowels are empty excreting your soul
What more can I give you baby I don't know
What more can I give you to make this thing grow
Don't turn your back now I'm talking to you
Should I pursue a path so twisted
Should I crawl defeated and gifted
Should I go the length of a river
The royal the throne the cry me river
Everything I've done I've done for you
Oh I give my life for you
Every move I made I move to you
And I came like a magnet for you now
What about it you're going to leave me
What about it you don't need me
What about it I can't live without you
What about it I never doubted you
What about it what about it
What about it what about it
Should I pursue a path so twisted
Should I crawl defeated and gifted
Should I go the length of a river
The royal the throne the cry me river
What about it what about it what about it
Oh I'm pissing in a river

Pumping (My Heart)

Oh I see you stare spiraling up there
Into the center of my brain and baby come baby go
And free the hurricane oh I go into the center of the airplane
Baby gotta move to the center of my pain
And my heart starts pumping my fists start pumping
Upset total abandon upset you know I love you so
Upset total abandon
Oh I see you stare spiraling up there and oh
Into the center of my brain and baby come baby go
And free the hurricane oh I go into the center of the airplane
Baby gotta box in the center of the ring
And my heart starts pumping my fists start pumping
Upset total abandon you know I love you so
Total abandon oh I go into the center of the airplane
Baby gotta go to the center of my brain
And my heart starts pumping my fists start pumping
Got no recollection of my past reflection
So I'm free to move in the resurrection
My heart starts pumping my fists start pumping
My heart pumping my heart pumping my heart pumping
Coming in the airport coming in the sea coming in the garden
Got a conscious stream coming in a washroom coming on a plane
Coming in a force field coming in my brain and my heart
My heart total abandon total abandon total abandon total
Abandon total abandon total abandon total abandon
Oh I go into the center of the airplane
Baby gotta move to the center of my brain
My heart

Distant Fingers

When when will you be landing
When when will you return
Feel feel my heart expanding
You and your alien arms

All my earthly dreams are shattered
I'm so tired I quit
Take me forever it doesn't matter
Deep inside of your ship
La la la la la la landing
Please oh won't you return
Feel see your blue lights are flashing
You and your alien arms

Deep in the forest I whirl
Like I did as a little girl
Let my eyes rise in the sky
Looking for you oh you know
I would go anywhere at all
Cause no star is too far with you
La la la la la la landing
Please oh won't you return
Feel feel my heart expanding
You and your alien arms

All my earthly dreams are shattered
I'm so tired I quit
Take me forever it doesn't matter
Deep inside of your ship
Land land oh I am waiting for you
Oh I am waiting for you oh I am waiting for you
Waiting for you to take me up by my starry spine
With your distant distant fingers
Oh I am waiting for you oh I am waiting for you

Chiklets

last night i awoke up from a dream came face to face with my
face facing the tombstone teeth of a man called chiklets he
came down through the ages with the desperate beauty of a
middleweight boxer came beating the force field with elegant
grace trying to get a perfect grip there was no absolute grip he
was in a sail boat a glass bottom boat the bottom of a boat he
was coming down through the ages sea molten sea spilling
down the tube the spiny eye of the village the spinal eye of
the victim the spiny eye like a question mark hovering over
him what do you want what do you want from him down on a
dream too much unexplained what do you think do you think
there was an actual connection i can't imagine a connection
going down there i can't imagine any connection at all a
boxing ring with gold ropes soft desperate karat top spinning
and coming down through the ages forty one BC

AUGUST 9, 1976. A hurricane coming on the city. New York boarded up like a rat house. Record Plant, Studio A. Aural aquarium for *Mermaid Turn the Tides 1985*. The air black. The wind whistling. Windows rattling. Jack Douglas stuffing rags beneath the doors, laying newspapers over the floor. Up above us, the moon was full. Setting up for the night of the Lion. The emblem of Ethiopia. The Kingdom of Sheba. The true earth of Rimbaud.

Nobody looked at each other but we were ready. The avenging starfish—we five in a circle. Unity was our drug. By the last take we were completely lost yet all there. My guitar felt fantastic in my hands. The neck like a mallot. My old brown amp swirling feedback like some ravaged violin. A storm was coming but I didn't feel nothing, just groping for the right note; the one that splits and sounds the alarm. A storm coming but I didn't feel nothing. Just me on my knees laughing hysterically, thankful for the privilege of playing in a rock and roll band.

notes, new york city, 1976

Radio Ethiopia/Abyssinia

Oh I'll send you a telegram
Oh I have some information for you
Oh I'll send you a telegram
Send it deep in the heart of you
Deep in the heart of your brain is a lever
Deep in the heart of your brain is a switch
Deep in the heart of your flesh you are clever
Oh you met your match in a bitch
There will be no famine in my existence
I merge with the people of the hills
People of Ethiopia
Your opiate is the air that you breathe
All those mint bushes around you
Are the perfect thing for your system
Aww clean clean it out
You must rid yourself from these these animal fixations
You must release yourself
From the thickening blackmail of elephantiasis
You must divide the wheat from the rats
You must turn around and look oh God
When I see Brancusi
His eyes searching out the infinite
Abstract spaces in the radio
Rude hands of sculptor
Now gripped around the neck of a Duo-Sonic
I swear on your eyes no pretty words will sway me

Ahh look at me look at the world around you
Jesus I hate to laugh but I can not believe
Care I so much everything merges then touch it
With a little soul anything is possible
Ahhh I never knew you how can it be
That I feel so fucked up
I am in no condition to do what I must do
The first dog on the street can tell you that
As for you you do as you must
But as for me I trust
That you will book me on the first freighter
Passage on the first freighter
So I can get the hell out of here
And go back home back to Abyssinia
Deep in the heart of the valley I'm going
Ohhh I would appreciate if you would just
Totally appreciate Brancusi's *Bird in Space*
The sculptor's mallet has been replaced
By the neck of a guitar
Lately
Every time I see your face
I eventually
wake up

F. T. G. F.

The New Year. 1977. Wearied by extensive touring, we prepared to go off the road. On our last date in Tampa, Florida, while performing "Ain't It Strange" on a high, poorly lit stage, I took a fall. My brother leaped off the stage to assist me, but I had fractured several vertebrae in my neck and spine.

The following months of recovery and rehabilitation were a difficult time for the band. But we stuck it out together. In this period I was able to resume my studies, reclaim my relationship with language, and with the assistance of Andi Ostrowe compile the work contained in *Babel*. It was in this period that the punk movement came to the forefront. It seemed to me that rock and roll was back on the streets, in the hands of the people. I trained, we regrouped and we joined them. And our bywords we gleaned from the scriptures, "Fight the good fight."

Easter

Use menace, use prayer.

—Jean Genet

Till Victory

Raise the sky, we got to fly
Over the land over the sea
Fate unwinds and if we die souls arise
God, do not seize me please. Till victory

Take arm. Take aim. Be without shame
No one to bow to. To vow to. To blame
Legions of light virtuous flight ignite excite
And you will see us coming
V formation through the sky
Film survives. Eyes cry. On the hill
Hear us call through a realm of sound
Oh oh-oh down and down
Down and round oh down and round
Round and round oh round and round

Rend the veil and we shall sail
The nail. The grail. That's all behind thee
In deed in creed the curve of our speed
And we believe that we will raise the sky
We got to fly over the land over the sea
Fate unwinds and if we die souls arise
God, do not seize me please. Till victory
Victory. Till victory. Victory. Till victory

WHILE recovering from my fall, I had time to contemplate what direction to take our work. I was studying the work of T. E. Lawrence, the New Testament, and the films of Pasolini. While watching *The Gospel According to St. Matthew*, I was struck by his commentary on Jesus as a revolutionary figure. I began to see him in another light—a teacher, a fighter, a guerrilla.

As we developed the material for *Easter*, these things were on my mind: the miracle of physical movement, the transmutation of energy through performance, and the idea of resurrection. Whether as a phoenix rising from the ashes or as a human being who just fell and got up again.

Easter was a stage of polarization. We had significant airplay as "Because the Night," co-written with Bruce Springsteen, rose up the charts. The album, which included "Rock n Roll Nigger," was deemed controversial. The redefining of an archaic slang term as a badge for those contributing on the fringe of society was not favorably embraced.

We took our hit and our "Rock n Roll Nigger" stance on the road. The group reassembled. My brother unfurled our colors. Andi repaired my faithful Duo-Sonic. And I packed my suitcase with my *Horses* jacket, the New Testament, and a tattered copy of *A Season in Hell*. For a time we were accompanied by Annie Liebovitz, who was shooting for *Rolling Stone*. Working with Annie was like working with a fellow band member. Looking through piles of her contact sheets, I was touched to find this shot of my beloved Swiss field boots. They had belonged to Jane Friedman's grandfather and, having survived many roads, have since been withdrawn from active service. I had worn my boots as we reentered the field with new health, new hope, and a renewed respect for the right and ability to do one's work.

Space Monkey

Blood on the TV ten o'clock news. Souls are invaded heart in a groove
Beating and beating so out of time what's the mad matter with the church chimes
Here comes a stranger up on Ninth Avenue leaning green tower indiscreet view
Over the cloud over the bridge sensitive muscle sensitive ridge
Of my space monkey sign of the time-time
Space monkey so out of line-line
Space monkey sort of divine and he's mine mine all mine

Pierre Clemente. Snortin' cocaine. The sexual streets why it's all so insane
Humans are running lavender room hovering liquid move over moon
For my space monkey sign of the time-time space monkey sort of divine
Space monkey so out of line and he's mine mine oh he's mine

Stranger comes up to him hands him an old rusty Polaroid
It starts crumbling in his hands. He says, oh man, I don't get the picture
This is no picture this is just this just a this just a . . . Just my jack-knife
Just my jack-knife just my jack-knife just my jack.

Rude excavation. Landing site. Boy hesitating jack-knife
He rips his leg open so out of time blood and light running
It's all like a dream light of my life he's dressed in flame
It's all so predestined it's all such a game
For my space monkey sign of the time-time
Space monkey sort of divine space monkey
So out of line and it's all just space just space

There he is up in a tree. Oh, I hear him calling down to me
That banana-shaped object ain't no banana
It's a bright yellow UFO and he's coming to get me
Here I go up up up up up up up up
Oh, good-bye mama I'll never do dishes again
Here I go from my body
Ha Ha Ha Ha Ha Ha
Help

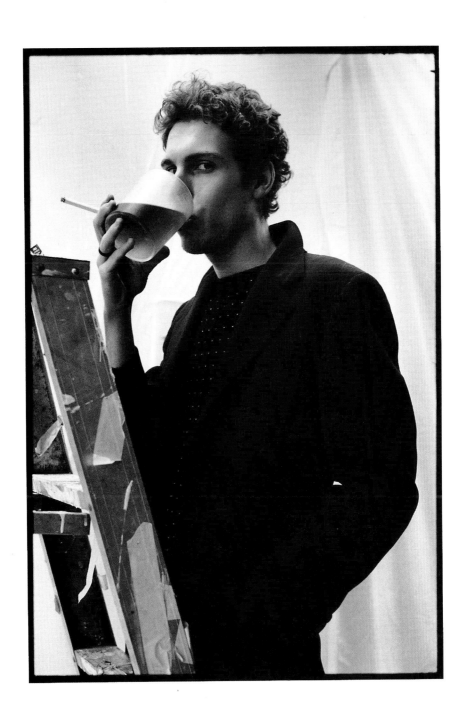

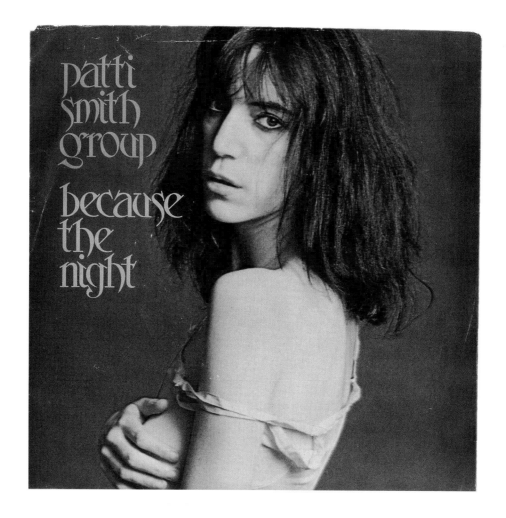

Easter was produced by an unheralded young engineer named Jimmy Iovine. In the course of our work he gave me a cassette of an unfinished song by his friend Bruce Springsteen. I resisted listening to it as we had already covered "Privilege" and I wanted the band members to write the balance of the songs. One restless night pacing my room, awaiting a phone call from Detroit, I spied the tape nestled among some beloved fragments of tattered cloth. I listened and was immediately struck by its anthemic quality. I finished the lyrics by dawn and presented it somewhat begrudgingly to the band. They unanimously agreed to record it. The result was a respectable hit single, a testament to Jimmy Iovine's vision and the cowriter's New Jersey heritage.

Because the Night

Take me now baby here as I am
Pull me close, try and understand
Desire is hunger is the fire I breathe
Love is a banquet on which we feed

Come on now try and understand
The way I feel when I'm in your hands
Take my hand come undercover
They can't hurt you now, can't hurt you now

Because the night belongs to lovers
Because the night belongs to love
Because the night belongs to lovers
Because the night belongs to us

Have I doubt when I'm alone
Love is a ring, the telephone
Love is an angel, disguised as lust
Here in our bed, until the morning comes

Come on now try and understand
The way I feel under your command
Take my hand as the sun descends
They can't touch you now, can't touch you now

And though we're seized with doubt
The vicious circle turns and burns
Without you I cannot live, forgive
The yearning burning, I believe it's time
To feel to heal, so touch me now,
touch me now, touch me now

Because this night there are two lovers
Because we believe in the night we trust
Because the night belongs to lovers
Because the night belongs to us

Ghost Dance

What is it children that falls from the sky
Tayi taya tayi aye aye
Manna from heaven from the most high
Food from the father tayi taya aye
We shall live again we shall live again
We shall live again shake out the ghost dance

Peace to your brother, give and take eat
Tayi taya dance little feet
One foot extended snake to the ground
Wave up the earth worm turn around
We shall live again we shall live again
We shall live again shake out the ghost dance

Stretch out your arms now dip and swing
Bird of thy birth tayi taya
The *oe* of the shoe the *ou* of the soul
Dust of the word that shakes from the tail
We shall live again we shall live again
We shall live again shake out the ghost dance

Here we are, Father, Lord, Holy Ghost
Bread of your bread host of your host
We are the tears that fall from your eyes
Word of your word cry of your cry
We shall live again we shall live again

What is it Father that turns to the right
What is it Father in your holy light
What is it Father that shakes from your hand
What is it Father that turns me around
What is it Father can you tell me when
Father, will we live again
We shall live again
We shall live again
We shall live again
Shake out the ghost

i haven't fucked much with the past, but i've fucked plenty with the future over the skin of silk are scars from the splinters of stations and walls i've caressed. a stage is like each bolt of wood, like a log of helen, is my pleasure. i would measure the success of a night by the way by the way by the amount of piss and seed i could exude over the columns that nestled the PA some nights i'd surprise everybody by skipping off with a skirt of green net sewed over with flat metallic circles which dazzled and flashed. the lights were violet and white i had an ornamental veil, but i couldn't bear to use it. when my hair was cropped i craved covering, but now my hair itself is a veil, and the scalp inside is a scalp of a crazy and sleepy comanche lies beneath this netting of the skin. i wake up. i am lying peacefully. i am lying peacefully and my knees are open to the sun. i desire him, and he is absolutely ready to seize me. in heart i am a moslem in heart i am an american. in heart i am moslem. in heart i'm an american artist and i have no guilt. i seek pleasure. i seek the nerves under your skin. the narrow archway; the layers; the scroll of ancient lettuce. we worship the flaw, the belly, the belly, the mole on the belly of an exquisite whore. he spared the child and spoiled the rod. i have not sold myself to god.

long at odds

Without question, Genet was one of the strangest literary figures of his time. In one of the great exchanges of the day, Jean-Paul Sartre wrote that Genet was a "liar, thief, pervert saint and martyr."

To which Genet replied, "I said it before, Sartre. It's true. So what?"

he was sent to a reformatory. There he vowed to reject the society that had so wronged him and to become what he was accused of being.

He specialized in stealing books.

There was an erotic thrill to thieving that exceeded the gratification he found in the humiliation of begging.

everything is shit.. the word ART must
be redefined. this is the age where
everybody creates.. rise up nigger take
up your true place.. rise up nigger the
word too must be redefined. this is
your arms and this is your hook.. donßt
the black boys get shook. high asses
asses get down. NIGGER no invented for
the color it was made for the plague.
for the royalty who have readjusted
their sores.. the artist. the mutant..
the rock and roll mulatto.. arise new
babe born sans eye-brow and tonsil..
outside logic beyond mathmatics
self torture and poli-tricks.. the
new science advances unknown geometry.
arise with new eyes new health health
new niggers.. this is your call your
calling your psalm. rise up niggers
and reign with your instruments
soldiers of new fortune. uncalcuable
caste of we new niggers.

MADE FOR the PLAGUE

Between books and prison stays, he
continued the cycle of theft, arrest,
prison and return to the streets.

By 1947, he had accumulated so
many convictions that under French
law he faced life imprisonment.

In the process, he became a saint of
sorts to the Beat Generation, produc-
ing literature of exotic beauty in the
mold of Charles Baudelaire, Sade,
Andre Gide and Arthur Rimbaud,

Rock n Roll Nigger

Baby was a black sheep baby was a whore
Baby got big and baby get bigger
Baby get something baby get more
Baby baby baby was a rock n roll nigger
Oh look around you all around you
Riding on a copper wave
Do you like the world around you
Are you ready to behave
Outside of society they're waiting for me
Outside of society that's where I want to be
Baby was a black sheep baby was a whore
You know she got big. Well she's gonna get bigger
Baby got a hand got a finger on the trigger
Baby baby baby is a rock n roll nigger
Outside of society that's where I want to be
Outside of society they're waiting for me
Those who have suffered understand suffering
And thereby extend their hand
The storm that brings harm
Also makes fertile blessed is the grass
And herb and the true thorn and light
I was lost in a valley of pleasure
I was lost in the infinite sea
I was lost and measure for measure
Love spewed from the heart of me
I was lost and the cost
And the cost didn't matter to me
I was lost and the cost was to be outside society
Jimi Hendrix was a nigger
Jesus Christ and grandma too
Jackson Pollock was a nigger
Nigger nigger nigger nigger
Nigger nigger nigger
Outside of society they're waitin' for me
Outside of society if you're looking
That's where you'll find me
Outside of society they're waitin' for me

The Lutheran bells were chiming at different intervals, woven together in the form of a round. The bells of Berlin.

Our encore. The people were shouting and pressing against the barricades. I glanced over to my brother leaning confidently against the bolted PA smoking a cigarette, clocking every movement within their movement. Everyone ready to erupt. The flag was flown. The metal horse was set to chomp. I could see the immense teeth. Electric blue tin. Neo-boys with electric hair. Pretty girls in bright pink sweaters. The children of Berlin.

We descended the stage and converged in a deserted lot behind the ballroom. We could hear the people stomping and calling out G L O R I A . . . They didn't sing with me. They waited 'til we left. The bells were chiming, the people chanting, and we headed for the wall. A hired car pulled into the lot, headlights flooding the area. A second followed suit. We entered them in silence and zeroed through the night.

It was black as shit. As instructed, we made our slow ascent up a long chain of metal stairs. In the distance, a slaughtered railway station and across was no-man's-land. The light of the headlamps revealed the wall—a vast span of whitewash—like a dream of Tom Sawyer. Only rebellious scrawls and anguished graffiti gave it the mean and shivery character it deserved.

All seemed moved. Why did I feel nothing? Adrenaline still rushing yet I was spent, beyond feeling. The sky was black save for a few embarrassed stars. I shut my eyes, conjuring late spring 1953. A crazy passage equaling death to some, separation to many.

I imagined a child letting go of a hand and the center of his world. I saw a couple waltzing before a great bay window swirling past cabinets of fine china, shining bone, brittle enamel and blue Dresden.

We all just stood there. Helplessly moved and removed by the expanse and pressure of history. The drivers were impatient. They signaled us with their lamps. The lights arrayed our faces, weary minstrels in blue coats and brown shoes. Comrades in the foolish and fragile depths of the severed city of Berlin.

notes, berlin, 1978

We Three

Every Sunday I would go down to the bar where he played guitar
You say you want me. I want another. Say you dream of me
Dream of your brother. Oh, the stars shine so suspiciously for we three
You said when you were with me that nothing made you high
We drank all night together and you began to cry so recklessly
Baby please don't take my hope away from me
You say you want me. I want another baby
You say you wish for me. Wish for your brother
Oh, the dice roll so deceptively for we three
It was just another Sunday and everything was in the key of A
And I lit a cigarette for your brother
And he turned and heard me say so desperately
Baby please don't take my hope away from me
You say you want me. I want another
You say you pray for me. Pray for your brother
Oh, the way that I see him is the way I see myself
So please stand back now and let time tell
Oh, can't you see that time is the key
That will unlock the destiny of we three
Every night on separate stars before we go to sleep we pray
So breathlessly. Baby please don't take my hope away from me

25th Floor

We explore the men's room
we don't give a shit
ladies lost electricity
take vows inside of it
desire to dance
too startled to try
wrap my legs round you
starting to fly
let's explore
up there up there up there
on the twenty-fifth floor

Circle all around me
coming for the kill kill kill
oh, kill me baby
like a kamikaze
heading for a spill
oh it's all spilt milk to me
desire to dance
too startled to try
wrap my legs round you
starting to fly let's soar
up there up there up there
on the twenty-fifth floor

We do not eat
flower of creation
we do not eat eat
anything at all
love is love was love is
a manifestation
I'm waiting for a contact or call
love's war. Love's cruel
love's pretty.
love's pretty cruel tonight
I'm waiting here to refuel
I'm gonna make contact tonight

Love in my heart
the night to exploit
twenty-five stories over Detroit
and there's more up there up there up there

Stoned in space. Zeus. Christ. It has always been rock and so it is and so it shall be
within the context of neo rock we must open up our eyes and seize and rend the veil
of smoke which man calls order. Pollution is a necessary result of the inability of man
to reform and transform waste.
the transformation of waste
the transformation of waste
the transformation of waste
the transformation of waste is perhaps the oldest preoccupation of man being the chosen
alloy he must be reconnected—via shit at all cost inherent within us is the dream of the
alchemist to create from the clay of man and to re-create from excretion of man pure and
then soft and then solid gold

All must not be art
Some art we must disintegrate
Positive
Anarchy
Must exist

what i feel when i'm playing guitar is completely cold and
crazy like i don't owe nobody nothing and it's just a test just to
see how far I can relax into the cold wave of a note when
everything hits just right the note of nobility can go on forever
i never tire of the solitary E and i trust my guitar and i don't
care about anything sometimes i feel like i've broken through
and i'm free and i could dig into eternity riding the wave and
realm of the E sometimes it's useless here I am struggling and
filled with dread afraid that i'll never squeeze enough graphite
from my damaged cranium to inspire or asphyxiate any eyes
grazing like hungry cows across the stage or page inside of me
i'm crazy i'm just crazy inside i must continue i see her my
stiff muse jutting around round round like a broken
speeding statue the colonial year is dead and the greeks too
are finished the face of alexander remains not only solely due
to sculpture but through the power and foresight and
magnetism of alexander himself the artist must maintain his
swagger he must be intoxicated by ritual as well as result look
at me i am laughing and i trust my guitar therefore we black
out together therefore i would run through scum and scum
is just ahead we see it but we just laugh we're ascending
through the hollow mountain we are peeking we are laughing
we are kneeling we are radiating at last this rebellion is just a
gas our gas that we pass

Godspeed

You are the adrenaline rushing through my veins
Stimulate my heart hailing crystalline
You are the sulfur extinguished by the flame
You are everything to me all is in your name

Walking in your blue coat weeping admiral
All the twisted sailors Vienna and Genet
Ended all that's static in a myth of sin
Mirror mine ecstatic pale adrenaline

Then you said to me it could never be
Set the owl to sea to see
And you said Godspeed

Love is a vampire energy undead
Love is like a boomerang it's gone and back again
On a raft of red leather on a raft of skin and sin
Tell me how to hail hail pale adrenaline

I'm walking follow me down the twisted stair
Stuck inside a memory shot and shot again
Hand upon a railing courting fate and fate
We're sailing sailing sailing down a black black river

And I plunge right in
And I plunge right in
Adrenaline adrenaline
Move inside my vein
Ah you're the speed I need
Throw the pistol in
Oh your love's a vampire
Coming in to suck
Stuck stuck stuck
Oh I fell and fell and fell
Down down down
Oh I'm going to
Duck duck duck

(Pas-de-Calais) — Vieux Calvaire sur la Route de

Easter

Easter Sunday we were walking
Easter Sunday we were talking
Isabelle, my little one
Take my hand time has come

Isabella, all is glowing
Isabella, all is knowing
And my heart, Isabella
And my head, Isabella

Frederic and Vitalie
Savior dwells inside of thee
Oh, the path leads to the sun
Brother sister time has come

Isabella, all is glowing
Isabella, all is knowing
Isabella, we are dying
Isabella, we are rising

I am the spring the holy ground
I am the seed of mystery
the thorn the veil the face of grace
the brazen image the thief of sleep
the ambassador of dreams
the prince of peace
I am the sword the wound the stain
Scorned transfigured child of Cain
I rend I end I return again
I am the salt the bitter laugh
I am the gas in a womb of light
The evening star the ball of sight
That bleeds that sheds the tears of Christ
Dying and drying as I rise tonight

Isabella, we are rising
Isabella, we are rising

Wave

I have fought a good fight, I have finished my course.

—Timothy 4:7

Frederick

Hi hello awake from thy sleep
God has given your soul to keep
All of the power that burns in the flame
Ignites the light in a single name
Frederick, name of care
Fast asleep in a room somewhere
Guardian angels lay abed
Shed their light on my sleepy head

High on a threshold yearning to sing
Down with the dancers having one last fling
Here's to the moment when you said hello
Come into my spirit are you ready let's go
Hi hi hey hey maybe I will
come back some day now
But tonight on the wings of a dove
Up above to the land of love

Now I lay me down to sleep
Pray the Lord my soul to keep
Kiss to kiss, breath to breath
My soul surrenders astonished to death
Night of wonder promise to keep
Set our sails channel the deep
Capture the rapture, two hearts meet
Minds entwined in a single beat

Frederick, you're the one
As we journey from sun to sun
All the dreams I waited so long for
Our flight tonight so long so long
Bye bye hey hey maybe
we will come back some day now
but tonight on the wings of a dove
Up above to the land of love

Frederick, name of care
High above with sky to spare
All the things I've been dreaming of
All expressed in this name of love

Dancing Barefoot

She is benediction
She is addicted to thee
She is the rude connection
She is connecting with he

Here I go and I don't know why
I feel so ceaselessly
Could it be he's taking over me

I'm dancing barefoot heading for a spin
Some strange music draws me in
Makes me come on like some heroine

She is sublimation
She is the essence of thee
She is concentrating on he
Who is chosen by she

I'm dancing barefoot heading for a spin
Some strange music draws me in
Makes me come on like some heroine

She is re-creation
She intoxicated by thee
She has the slow sensation
That he is levitating with she

Here I go and I don't know why
I spin so ceaselessly
Till I lose my sense of gravity

I'm dancing barefoot heading for a spin
Some strange music draws me in
Makes me come on like some heroine

The plot of our life sweats in the dark like a face
The mystery of childbirth, of childhood itself
Grave visitations; what is it that calls to us
Why must we pray screaming
Why must not death be redefined
We shut our eyes
We stretch out our arms
And whirl on a pane of glass
An afixiation a fix on anything
The line of life the limb of tree
The hands of he
The promise that she
Is blessed among women

Oh god, I fell for you

Revenge

I feel upset. Let's do some celebrating
Come on honey don't hesitate now
Needed you. You withdrew. I was so forsaken
Ah, but now the tables have turned. My move
I believe I'll be taking my revenge. Sweet revenge

I thought you were some perfect read-out. Some digital delay
Had obscured and phased my view of the wicked hand you played
The sands and hands of time have run out. Run out
You better face it this thing's run amok. This luck
I do know how to replace it with revenge. Sweet revenge

I gave you a wristwatch baby
You wouldn't even give me the time of day
You want to know what makes me tick
Now it's me that's got precious little to say
For the ghosts of our love have dried have died
There's no use faking it
The spirits going to close in on you tonight
High time I was taking my revenge
Sweet revenge. Revenge. Revenge

All the gold and silver couldn't measure
Up my love for you. It's so immaterial
I wouldn't wait around if I were you
In the valley of wait-ting ting
Nobody gets nothing. Nobody gets anything. No
No time for kisses
Don't leave me no space in your little boat
You ain't going to need, no you ain't going to need no little boat
You are living on marked time my dear. Revenge. Sweet revenge.
Sweet, sweet revenge.

Citizen Ship

It was nothing. It didn't matter to me
There were tanks all over my city
There was water outside the windows
And children in the streets were throwing rocks at tanks
Ain't got a passport ain't got my real name
Ain't got a chance sport at fortune or fame
As I walk these endless streets won't you give me a lift
A lift a lift on your citizen ship
They were rioting in Chicago movement in L.A.
'68 it broke the Yardbirds. We were broke as well
Took it underground. M.C. borderline. Up against the wall
The wall. The wall. Show your papers boy
Citizen ship we got memories. Stateless they got shame
Cast adrift from the citizen ship lifeline denied exiled this castaway
Blind alley in New York City in a foreign embrace
If you're hungry you're not too particular about what you'll taste
Men in uniform gave me vinegar spoon of misery
But what the hell I fell I fell. It doesn't matter to me
Citizen ship we got memories. Citizen ship we got pain
Cast adrift from the citizen ship lifeline denied exile this castaway
I was caught up like a moth with its wings out of sync
Cut the cord. Overboard. Just a refugee
Lady liberty lend a hand to me I've been cast adrift
Adrift. Adrift. Adrift. Adrift. Adrift. Adrift
On the citizen ship we got memory. Citizen ship we got pain
Lose your grip on the citizen ship you're cast you're cast away
On the citizen ship you got memory. Citizen ship you got pain
Citizen ship you got identity. A name a name a name
A name. Ivan. A name. Ivan Kral. Name. Name.
What's your name son. New York City. What's your name.
What's your name. What's your name. Name. Nothing.
I got nothing. Name. Name. Name. Name. Wake up
New Jersey. Give me your tired your poor. Give me your huddled masses
Your war torn on your tender seas. Give me your war torn
On your shores of dawn. Lift up your golden lamp for me.
Ahh, it's all mythology

Seven Ways of Going

I've got seven ways of going seven wheres to be
Seven sweet disguises, seven ways of serving Thee
Lord, I do extol Thee for Thou hast lifted me
Woke me up and shook me out of mine iniquity
For I was undulating in the lewd impostered night
Steeped in a dream to rend the seams to redeem the rock of right

Swept through the seas of Galilee and the Seven Hills of Rome
Seven sins were wrung from the sight of me
Lord, I turned my neck toward home
I opened up my arms to you and we spun from life to life
'Til you loosened me and let me go toward the everlasting light

In this big step I am taking seven seizures for the true
I got seven ways of going seven ways of serving you
As I move through seven levels as I move upon the slate
As I declare to you the number of my moves as I speculate
The eighth seeking love without exception a light upon the swarm
Seeking love without exception a saint in any form

Broken Flag

Nodding though the lamp's lit low. Nod for passers underground
To and fro she's darning and the land is weeping red and pale
Weeping yarn from Algiers. Weeping yarn from Algiers

Weaving though the eyes are pale. What will rend will also mend
The sifting cloth is binding and the dream she weaves will never end
For we're marching toward Algiers. For we're marching toward Algiers

Lullaby though baby's gone. Lullaby a broken song
Oh, the cradle was our call. When it rocked we carried on
And we marched on toward Algiers. For we're marching toward Algiers
We're still marching for Algiers. Marching, marching for Algiers

Not to hail a barren sky. The sifting cloth is weeping red
The mourning veil is waving high a field of stars and tears we've shed
In the sky a broken flag. Children wave and raise their arms
We'll be gone but they'll go on and on and on and on and on

In the fall of 1979, the Patti Smith Group prepared to close up shop. No fanfare, no farewell; we just did our jobs, then went on our way. Our last shows were in Bologna and Florence. Not by design, just chance. We were greeted by paparazzi, a new pope, and a volatile political situation beyond our scope.

They were waiting for us in the hotel lobby, desperate dispatchers of this cause and that, gripping our sleeves and beseeching us to use any influence they imagined we had. To free political prisoners, to reinforce the fringe. Intellectuals, gumshoes, and weeping women. Live TV crews surrounded us. The crew spoke little English and I no Italian. A perfect recipe for the failure to communicate.

The poet Gregory Corso had joined our caravan. He blasphemed, he Blaked, and now he translated their requests. Use the media, he winked to me, and I did, spitting out the needs of the people, Mickey Spillane style. Some onlookers gasped at this use of the Italian media, but it was no risk to me. Just another ugly American, just a novice moving through a convoluted revolution, just a weary rock and roll singer's last stand.

The TV crew seemed oblivious. Gregory seemed violently amused. People surrounded us with flags and flyers and manifestos. It was hard to convey that we truly could not fight their battles, only salute them. We had our own seemingly insignificant battle; small in the scheme of things, honor-bound to play out. A small sports arena in the middle of nowhere. Signifying nothing but the end of the line for a rock and roll band. I passed through heavily armed security. We had our own fight.

I got a call from Ina Meibach, who represented us. The flag, she said, it could be dangerous to raise. I went over her words. Our guitarist Ivan Kral was a political refugee. We were playing a communist venue. We had bomb threats, life threats. High-minded hotheads that hated America.

I sent for my brother. He was guardian of the flag. He raised and lowered it; folded it and tied it up. All with mute respect. I told him as I had been told. He lit a cigarette and looked down. "It's your call," I said. "I'll back it."

"Let's raise it," he said.
"Let's raise hell."

notes, bologna, 1979

Wave

Hi. Hi. I was running after you for a long time. I was watching you for . . . actually I've watched you for a long time. I like to watch you when you're walking back and forth on the beach. And the way your, the way your cloth looks. I like I like to see the edges, the bottom of it get all wet when you're walking near the water there. It's real nice to talk to you. I didn't. I-I-I-I. How are you? How are you? I saw I saw you from your balcony window and you were standing there waving at everybody. It was really great because there was about a billion people there, but when I was waving to you, the way your face was, it was so, the way your face was, it made me feel exactly like we're, it's not that you were just waving to me, but that we were we were waving to each other. Really it was really wonderful. I really felt happy. It really made me happy. And. Um. I. I just wanted to thank you because you, you really really you made me feel good and, oh, I, it's nothing. Well I'm just clumsy. No, it's just a Band-Aid. No, it's OK. Oh no, I'm always doing. Something's always happening to me. Well. I'll be seeing you. Good-bye. Bye. Good-bye sir. Good-bye papa.

Wave thou art pretty
Wave thou art high
Wave thou art music
Wave thou art why
Wave thou art pretty
Wave thou art high
Wave to the city
Wave wave good-bye
Wave thou art high
Wave thou art pretty
Wave to the children
Wave good-bye

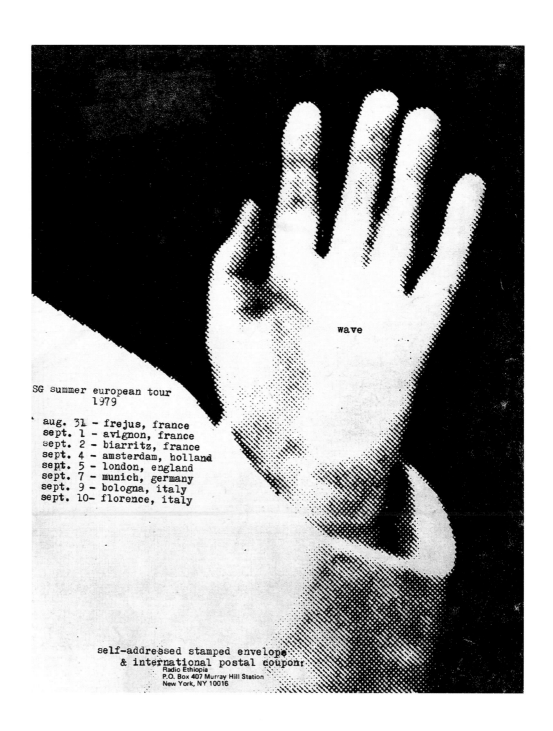

wave

SG summer european tour
    1979

aug. 31 - frejus, france
sept. 1 - avignon, france
sept. 2 - biarritz, france
sept. 4 - amsterdam, holland
sept. 5 - london, england
sept. 7 - munich, germany
sept. 9 - bologna, italy
sept. 10- florence, italy

self-addressed stamped envelope
  & international postal coupon
Radio Ethiopia
P.O. Box 407 Murray Hill Station
New York, NY 10016

FLORENCE was our last job. We arrived and I hit the streets, looking for the slaves of Michelangelo. There were thousands of kids camped in the alleyways. What the hell was going on? I passed a newsstand and saw my face on the cover of every other magazine. Spotted by scores of screaming girls in shirts and ties, I scooted down the back streets to the Hotel Minerva. I holed up there for hours, downing espresso.

Our last job. In a soccer arena. Miles from Michelangelo. I got there and discovered I had forgotten my shirt and tie and my only pair of socks. I was dressed beatnik style—ponytail, boatneck, boots with no socks. I needed a pair badly. Our sound guy volunteered his. My brother delivered them, some kind of red wool hunting socks. I gave Todd two cassettes to play before us. Jean Paul I speaking to school children, which they booed. Beethoven's *Third Symphony Eroica*, second movement, which they booed. And then ourselves, which they did not.

We did our work. We finished our course. The people moved forward. It was our last "My Generation." I remembered the first time we performed it in Cleveland, Ohio, crying out, "We created it, let's take it over!" I solicited them to do the same. They ascended upon us. I gave up my guitar. Jay gave over his drums. Joyful anarchy erupted and we sanctioned it. The cries through my microphone and the discordant music was their own. I turned all the amps up to ten, saluted my brother, and said goodbye.

Later, I returned the socks to Carl, our sound guy.
"How was it?" I said.
"Oh my God!" was all he could say.
"What did it look like?"
"Like human waves," he said, "like waves."
"Yeah," I said, "as it should be, like waves."

My brother folded and bound our flag, retiring it from duty. I then set out for my new life. I could not toss my trusty jacket over my shoulder, Sinatra style, as it had been stolen several months before in Chicago, the city of my birth.

notes, florence, 1979

Hymn

When I am troubled in the night
He comes to comfort me
He wills me thru the darkness
And the empty child is free
To take his hand his sacred heart
The heart that breaks the dawn
Amen. And when I think
I've had my fill he fills up again

Dream of Life

Peace, peace! he is not dead, he doth not sleep—
He hath awakened from the dream of life—

—Percy Bysshe Shelley

ONE afternoon while performing KP duties, I was interrupted by Fred with these words, "People have the power. Write it." After scraping out the pots and pans, I set about my studies in preparation for writing the lyrics. The next few weeks were spent listening to the Reverend Jesse Jackson speak and going over several Bible verses with my sister Linda. Weaving these references with a dream of the shepherds of Afghanistan and their Russian invaders calling truce and resting peacefully together beneath the work of God, I wrote the words and gave them to Fred.

This song became our anthem for *Dream of Life*. This was an extremely difficult album to create, with two highly self-critical people trying to please themselves as well as each other. We were aided by the patient and supportive Richard Sohl, who came to work with us for some months prior to recording. His sense of humor, his classical knowledge, and our long history enabled us to realize our efforts, bringing them out of exile into the world.

People Have the Power

I was dreaming in my dreaming
Of an aspect bright and fair
And my sleeping it was broken
But my dream it lingered near
In the form of shining valleys
Where the pure air recognized
And my senses newly opened
I awakened to the cry
That the people have the power
To redeem the work of fools
Upon the meek the graces shower
It's decreed the people rule

The people have the power
The people have the power
The people have the power
The people have the power

Vengeful aspects became suspect
And bending low as if to hear
And the armies ceased advancing
Because the people had their ear
And the shepherds and the soldiers
Lay beneath the stars
Exchanging visions
And laying arms
To waste in the dust
In the form of shining valleys
Where the pure air recognized
And my senses newly opened
I awakened to the cry

The people have the power
The people have the power
The people have the power
The people have the power

Where there were deserts
I saw fountains
Like cream the waters rise
And we strolled there together
With none to laugh or criticize
And the leopard
And the lamb
Lay together truly bound
I was hoping in my hoping
To recall what I had found
I was dreaming in my dreaming
God knows a purer view
As I surrender to my sleeping
I commit my dream to you

The people have the power
The people have the power
The people have the power
The people have the power

The power to dream to rule
To wrestle the world from fools
It's decreed the people rule
It's decreed the people rule
Listen. I believe everything we dream
Can come to pass through our union
We can turn the world around
We can turn the earth's revolution

We have the power
People have the power

Up There Down There

Up there
There's a ball of fire
Some call it the spirit
Some call it the sun
Its energies are not for hire
It serves man it serves everyone
Down there where Jonah wails
In the healing water
In the ready depths
Twisting like silver swans
No line of death no boundaries

Up there
The eye is hollow the eye is winking
The winds ablaze angels howling
The sphinx awakens
But what can she say
You'd be amazed
Down there
Your days are numbered
Nothing to fear
There will be trumpets
There will be silence
In the end the end
Will be here just here

Ahh the borders of heaven
Are zipped up tight tonight
The abstract streets
The lights like some switched-on Mondrian
Cats like us are obsolete
Hey Man don't breathe on my feet
Thieves, poets we're inside out
And everybody's a soldier
Angels howl at those abstract lights
And the borders of heaven
Are zipped up tight tonight

Up there
There's a ball of fire
Some call it the spirit
Some call it the sun
Its energies are not for hire
It serves man it serves everyone
The air we breathe
The flame of wisdom
The earth we grind
The beckoning sea
It's no mystery
Not sentimental
Ahh the equation
It's all elemental

The world is restless
Heaven in flux
Angels appear
From the bright storm
Out of the shadows
Up there, down there
But what can we say
Man's been forewarned

All communion is not holy
Even those that fall
They can prophet understanding
It's all for man
It's for everyone
It's up there, down there
Everywhere
Everywhere
Time for communion
Time for communion
Talking communion

Paths That Cross

For Samuel J. Wagstaff, Jr. (1921–1987)

Speak to me
Speak to me heart
I feel a needing
To bridge the clouds
Softly go
A way I wish to know to know
A way I wish to know to know

Oh you'll ride
Surely dance in a ring
Backwards and forwards
Those who seek
Feel the glow
A glow we all will know
A glow we all will know

On that day filled with grace
And the heart's communion
Steps we take steps we trace
Into the light of reunion

Paths that cross
Will cross again
Paths that cross
Will cross again

Speak to me
Speak to me shadow
I spin from the wheel
Nothing at all save the need
The need to weave
A silk of souls
That whisper whisper
A silk of souls
That whispers to me

Speak to me heart
All things renew
Hearts will mend
'Round the bend
Paths that cross
Cross again
Paths that cross
Will cross again

Rise up hold the reins
We'll meet again
I don't know when
Hold tight bye bye
Paths that cross
Will cross again
Paths that cross
Will cross again

Somalia

I don't know why I feel this way today
The sky is blue the table is laid
The trees are heavy with yellow fruit
And in their shade children happily play

The pears have fallen to the ground
My child places one in my hand
The sun is warm upon my face
And I dream of a burning land

Mother of famine take this pear
Upon an arrow through the rings of time
This small fruit this golden prayer
May it pass from this hand to thine

If I were rain I'd rain on Somalia
If I were grain for Somalia I'd grow
If I were bread I would rise for Somalia
If I were a river for Somalia I'd flow

All the mothers will dream of thee
All the mothers bless thy empty hand
All the mothers will grieve for thee
All the sorrow a mother can stand

If we were rain we would rain for Somalia
If we were grain for Somalia we'd grow
If we were bread we would rise for Somalia
If we were a river for Somalia we'd flow

*—This lyric was written in memory of Audrey Hepburn,
who worked with the simple industry of a servant to give
comfort to the victims of the famine in Somalia.*

Wild Leaves

Wild leaves are falling
Falling to the ground
Every leaf a moment
A light upon the crown
That we'll all be wearing
In a time unbound
And wild leaves are falling
Falling to the ground

Every word that's spoken
Every word decreed
Every spell that's broken
Every golden deed
All the parts we're playing
Binding as the reed
And wild leaves are falling
Wild wild leaves

The spirits that are mentioned
The myths that have been shorn
Everything we've been through
And the colors worn
Every chasm entered
Every story wound
And wild leaves are falling
Falling to the ground

As the campfire's burning
As the fire ignites
All the moments turning
In the stormy bright
Well enough the churning
Well enough believe
The coming and the going
Wild wild leaves

Dream of Life

I'm with you always
You're ever on my mind
In a light to last a whole life through
Each way I turn the sense of you surrounds
In every step I take in all I do
Your thoughts your schemes
Captivate my dreams
Everlasting ever new
Sea returns to sea
And sky to sky
In a life of dream am I
When I'm with you

Deep in my heart
How the presence of you shines
In a light to last a whole life through
I recall the wonder of it all
Each dream of life I'll share with you
Sea returns to sea
And sky to sky
In a life of dream am I
When I'm with you

I'm with you always
You're ever on my mind
In a light to last a whole life through
The hand above turns those leaves of love
All and all a timeless view
Each dream of life
Flung from paradise
Everlasting ever new

Dream of Life
Dream of Life

Where Duty Calls

In a room in Lebanon
They silently slept
They were dreaming crazy dreams
In a foreign alphabet
Lucky young boys
Cross on the main
The driver was approaching
The American zone
The waving of hands
The tiniest train
They never dreamed
They'd never wake again

Voice of the Swarm
We follow we fall
Some kneel for priests
Some wail at walls
Flag on a match head
God or the law
And they'll all go together
Where duty calls

United children
Child of Iran
Parallel prayers
Baseball Koran
I'll protect mama
I'll lie awake
I'll die for Allah
In a holy war
I'll be a ranger
I'll guard the streams
I'll be a soldier
A sleeping marine

In the heart of the ancient
Ali smiles
In the soul of the desert
The sun blooms awake
Into the glare of all our little wars
Who pray to return to salute
The coming and dying of the moon
Oh sleeping sun

Assassin in prayer
Laid a compass deep
Exploding dawn
And himself as well
Their eyes for his eyes
Their breath for his breath
All to his end

And a room in Lebanon
Dust of scenes
Erase and blend
May the blanket of kings
Cover them and him

Forgive them Father
They know not what they do
From the vast portals
Of their consciousness
They're calling to you

—*This was written in memory of those who lost their lives in the destruction of the First Battalion, 8th Marine Headquarters, Beirut, October 23, 1983. Two hundred and forty-one marines, sailors, and soldiers on a peacekeeping mission perished with their assassin.*

Going Under

Sun is rising on the water
Light is dancing again
Let's go under where the sun beams
Let's go under my friend
Are we sleeping
Are we dreaming
Are we dancing again
Is it heaven crack it open
And we'll slide down its stream
We can hold on [I'm sure]
To the sea's foaming mane
It will serve us
We'll surface
And we'll plunge back again
Sun is rising on the water
Light is dancing like a flame
There's no burning where the sun beams
Oh it's such a lovely game
Does the sea dream [I'm sure]
We are here, we attend
We are bells on the shore
As the tolling suspends
Who will decide the shape of things
The shift of being
Who will perceive when life is new
Shall we divide and become another
Who is due for gift upon gift
Who will decide
Shall we swim over and over
The curve of a wing
Its destination ever changing
Sun is rising on the water
Light is dancing like a flame
Let's go waltzing on the water
Let's go under again
Let's go under
Going under

As the Night Goes By

Darlin' come under cover
Another night to discover
Let's slip where senses gather
Let's drift between the sea and sky
As the night goes by

Sands shift
Orchids so strange
In the moonlight
Brushing our faces
Places where love blooms
And dies
While the night goes by
Oh, and the spirits call
Sun upon your shadows fall
Tracing every breath we draw

Come into my dreams
Come into my dreams
Darlin' let's go where the night goes
Let's drift where senses gather
Let's make this night last forever
Into my dreams
Into my dreams

Darlin' let's go
Where the night goes
Time slips
Oh darlin' how it flies
When the night goes by

All through the night
Sirens call
Come to me
I'll come to you
As the night softly
goes by bye

Midnight
Moon on our shoulder
Daybreak
Another one older
Darlin' heavenly blue
Glories fade into view

Let's go
Under the stars
That are beating
Under the moonlight
Stars shoot
Dusk just a whisper
Make this night
Last forever
Oh how I wonder
Where the night goes
Oh let's wonder
Where the night goes
As the night goes
By bye
By bye

Looking for You (I Was)

In the medieval night
'Twas love's design
And the sky was open
Like a valentine
All the lacy lights
Where wishes fall
And like Shakespeare's child
I wished on them all

Ahh to be your destiny
Was all that I pursued
I could see the sights
From the lofty heights
But my heart obscured the view

I was looking for you
Looking for you
What could I do
I was looking for you

Along the black river
The ambassador jewels
And you were reflected
In all that I saw
In the towers of gold
In the wheel and wing
Gripping my senses
Like an ancient claim

Many is the time I knelt in the light
Appealing to all that I know
Guide my eyes and steps
That I may find love true

I was looking for you
Looking for you
What could I do
I was looking for you

Come on darlin'
All that hearts desire
Was written before us
In the medieval fire
It was love's design
In the glittering stars
Like Shakespeare's child
To be where you are

From the Portobello Road
To the Port of Marseilles
Where the dervish turns
Where the wild goats play

Looking for you
I was

In the process of recording *Dream of Life*, Robert photographed me for my fortieth birthday. He handed me a blue Morpheus butterfly, a symbol for transformation. He photographed me in my braids, in Burbank, California, in full sun, three months before the birth of my daughter Jesse. The following winter our family portrait was taken in his studio in New York City. This family portrait marked the last time that I was to be photographed by my great friend.

Robert came to the studio when we recorded "The Jackson Song." He was not well, and he lay down on the couch in the control room. Richard sat at the grand piano, and I sat opposite him. Fred came over to Richard and said simply, "Make them cry." We performed it twice. The second take was as good as we were able to do. When we finished, I looked at Richard, and he smiled. I looked through the glass and saw that Robert was sleeping peacefully as Fred stood by him, silently weeping.

The Jackson Song

Little blue dreamer go to sleep
Let's close our eyes and call the deep
Slumbering land that just begins
When day is done and little dreamers spin

First take my hand then let it go
Little blue boy you're on your own
Little blue wings as those feet fly
Little blue shoes that walk across the sky

May your path be your own
But I'm with you
And each day you'll grow
He'll be there too
And someday you'll go
We'll follow you
As you go, as you go

Little blue star that offers light
Little blue bird that offers flight
Little blue path where those feet fall
Little blue dreamer won't you dream it all

May your path be your own
But I'm with you
And each day you'll grow
He'll be there too
And someday you'll go
We'll follow you
As you go, as you go

And in your travels you will see
Warrior wings remember Daddy
And if a mama bird you see
Folding her wings will you remember me
As you go, as you go, as you go, as you go

Memorial Song

Little emerald bird
Wants to fly away
If I cup my hand
Could I make him stay

Little emerald soul
Little emerald eye
Little emerald soul
Must you say good-bye

All the things that we pursue
All that we dream are composed
As nature knew in a feather green
Little emerald bird

As you light afar it is true I heard
God is where you are little emerald soul
Little emerald eye little emerald bird
We must say good-bye

ROBERT MAPPLETHORPE

November 4, 1946 – March 9, 1989

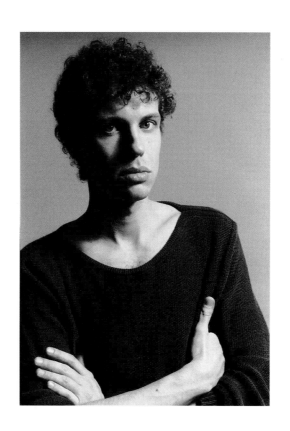

RICHARD ARTHUR SOHL

May 26, 1954 — June 3, 1990

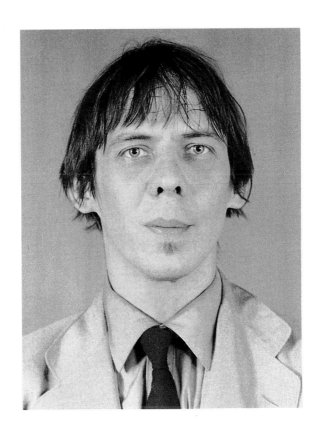

Frederick D. Smith

Twentieth Century

ON Thanksgiving Day in 1994, my family gathered in South Jersey at the home of my parents. It was a dark time for me and it was good to be with them. Saturday morning my brother Todd wrapped his coat around me and took me for a drive. He rolled the windows down, started up a tape of "Rock n Roll Nigger" full volume and sang along, cajoling me to join him. We flew along the road, landing, as I thought we might, before a revered landmark of our childhood, Thomas's Field. Overgrown yet radiantly holy, encompassing all our passionate play and still graced by Hoedown Hall where we had danced on summer evenings.

"You're gonna make it," he said, "and I'll be there. You'll do new work and take it to the people and I'll be right by your side." He stood there grinning, his pale blue eyes squinting in the November sun, the ever-present cigarette hanging loose off his lip.

We stood before the place that witnessed all our valiant wars. He always let me be the leader, as he would now if I returned to the field.
"I'll be there," he said.
And I knew he would. And I also knew, as I looked up at him, who was the better man.

Todd Pollard Smith

June 15, 1949 – December 4, 1994

Gone Again

Thou hast turned for me my mourning into dancing.

—Psalm 30:11

FRED and I began to chart the territory for another album in 1994. Fred, as was his method, offered titles and concepts for me to develop lyrically. "Summer Cannibals" was to address the darker side of being a rock musician. Vampiristic energies which provide no energy at all. He drew from his Indian heritage to form "Gone Again." He chanted sketches of a melody on a work tape. He saw the song from the point of view of a tribe's shaman. An old woman comes down from the hills to account to her people their history, reaffirming to them, in time of strife, the cycle of life and the changing seasons.

I came to him one evening and expressed my desire to learn to play the acoustic guitar so I could write songs of my own. He said he would teach me if I would practice hard. He kept his word and gave me lessons. I was a slow pupil, but he was a patient, encouraging teacher.

I brought him a little song I wrote when Jackie Kennedy died. Fred was taken with it and often sang and played it himself while I sang harmonies on the chorus. I was proud that he, a prolific and gifted musician, would like my song so much. Fred's health deteriorated that year and we spent less time writing songs. Instead, he would have me sit and practice my chords and we'd end with "She Walked Home."

> She traced the clouds
> that formed above her adventures
> they billowed and fell
> like a shroud in her hand
> she knew she was not very well
> she realized she would never
> trace them again
> she walked home

Fred and I never recorded again, for he passed away in November. But the Lord who taketh away also giveth. In February 1995 Allen Ginsberg called to offer his condolences with the words, "Let go of the spirit of the departed and continue your life's celebration." He encouraged me to join him in his efforts to benefit the Tibetan Buddhist community. Having an awareness of the plight of the Dalai Lama and his people, I gratefully accepted.

On February 16, 1995, we performed together for the Jewel Heart Organization at the State Theater in Ann Arbor, Michigan. We were greeted warmly by Gelek Rinpoche, and a strong bond was created between us. On that same evening I met the poet Oliver Ray.

Oliver Ray inspired me to continue working. Lenny Kaye was instrumental in drawing together a new work force. He pieced together the songs Fred had left behind. With Oliver, Jay Dee Daugherty, Tony Shanahan, Tom Verlaine, and Malcolm Bern we began the recording process, choosing Electric Lady, where *Horses* had been recorded. There we created *Gone Again* in Fred's memory.

I did not have the heart to record "She Walked Home." Somehow Fred had made it his own. But as a remembrance I set a photograph of a young smiling Jacqueline Bouvier on my music stand.

Gone Again

Hey now man's own kin
We commend into the wind
Grateful arms grateful limbs
Grateful soul he's gone again

I have a winter's tale
How vagrant hearts relent prevail
Sow their seed into the wind
Seize the sky and they're gone again

Fame is fleeting god is nigh
We raise our arms to him on high
We shoot our flint into the sun
We bless our spoils and we're gone we're gone

Hey now man's own kin
We commend into the wind
Grateful arms grateful limbs
Grateful heart he's gone again

Here a man, man's own kin
Turned his back and his own people shot him
And he fell on his knees
Before the burning plain
And he beheld fields of gold his land his son
And he arose his blood aflame
Clouds pressed with hand prints stained

One last breath
The sky is high
The hungry earth
The empty vein
The ashes rain
Death's own bed
Man's own kin
Into the wind
One last breath
Hole in life
Love knot tied
Braid undone
A child born
The hollow horn
A warrior cried
A warrior died
One last breath
Lick of flame
Spirit moaned
Spirit shed
The heavens fed
Man's own kin
Grips the sky
And he's gone again

Hey now man's own kin
We lay down into the wind
Grateful arms grateful limbs
Grateful heart is gone again

Hey now man's own kin
He ascends into the wind
Grateful arms grateful limbs
Grateful man he's gone again

Beneath the Southern Cross

Oh to be
Not anyone
Gone
This maze of being
Skin.
Oh to cry
Not any cry
So mournful that
The dove
Just laughs
And the steadfast
Gasps
Oh to owe
Not anyone
Nothing
To be
Not here
But here
Forsaking
Equatorial bliss
Who walked through
The callow mist
Dressed in scraps
Who walked
The curve of the world
Whose bone scraped
Whose flesh unfurled
Who grieves not
Anyone gone
To greet lame
The inspired sky
Amazed to stumble
Where gods get lost
Beneath
The southern cross

About a Boy

Toward another he has gone
To breathe an air beyond his own
Toward a wisdom beyond the shelf
Toward a dream that dreams itself
About a boy beyond it all
About a boy beyond it all

From the forest from the foam
From the field that he had known
Toward a river twice as blessed
Toward the inn of happiness
About a boy beyond it all
About a boy beyond it all

From a chaos raging sweet
From the deep and dismal street
Toward another kind of peace
Toward the great emptiness
About a boy beyond it all
About a boy beyond it all

I stood among them I listened
I stood among them I listened not
I stood among them and I heard myself
Who I've loved better than you
So much so that I walked on
Into the face of God
Away from your world
And my sour stomach
Into the face of God, who said
Boy, I knew thee not, but boy
Now that I have you in my face
I embrace you. I welcome you
He was just a boy
Whirling in the snow
Just a little boy
Who would never grow

My Madrigal

We waltzed beneath motionless skies
All heaven's glory turned in your eyes
We expressed such sweet vows

Oh till death do us part
Oh till death do us part

We waltzed beneath God's point of view
Knowing no ending to our rendezvous
We expressed such sweet vows

Oh till death do us part
Oh till death do us part

We waltzed beneath motionless skies
All heaven's glory turned in your eyes
You pledged me your heart
Till death do us part
You pledged me your heart
Till death do us part

Till death do us part

Summer Cannibals

I was down in Georgia
Nothing was as real
As the street beneath my feet
Descending into air

The cauldron was a'bubbling
The flesh was lean
And the women moved forward
Like piranhas in a stream
They spread themselves before me
An offering so sweet
And they beckoned
And they beckoned
Come on darling eat

Eat the summer cannibals
Eat Eat Eat
You eat the summer cannibals
Eat Eat Eat

They circled around me
Natives in a ring
And I saw their souls a'withering
Like snakes in chains
And they wrapped themselves around me
Ummm what a treat
And they rattled their tales
hissing come on let's eat

Eat the summer cannibals
Eat Eat Eat
You eat the summer cannibals
Eat Eat Eat

I felt a rising in my throat
The girls a'saying grace
And the air the vicious air
Pressed against my face
And it all got too damn much for me
Just got too damn rough
And I pushed away my plate
And said boys I've had enough
And I laid upon the table
Just another piece of meat
And I opened up my veins to them
And said come on eat

Eat the summer cannibals
Eat Eat Eat
You eat the summer cannibals
Eat Eat Eat

'Cause I was down in Georgia
Nothing was as real
As the street beneath my feet
Descending into hell
So Eat Eat Eat
Eat Eat Eat

Dead to the World

Dead to the world my body was sleeping
On my mind was nothing at all
Come a mist an air so appealing
I'm here a whisper you summoned I called
I formed me a presence whose aspect was changing
Oh he would shift he would not shift at all
We sat for a while he was very engaging
And when he was gone I was gone on a smile

With a strange way of walking
And a strange way of breathing
More lives than a cat
That led me astray
All in all he captured my heart
Dead to the world and I just
Slipped away

I heard me a music that drew me to dancing
Lo I turned under his spell
I opened my coat but he never came closer
I bolted the door and I whispered oh well
I laid in the rushes the air was upon me
Wondering well I just couldn't discern
Will he come back come back to me
Oh I whispered will you ever return

I was feeling sensations in no dictionary
He was less than a breath of shimmer and smoke
The life in his fingers unwound my existence
Dead to the world alive I awoke

With a strange way of walking
And a strange way of breathing
Less than a breath of shimmer and smoke
The life in his fingers unwound my existence
Dead to the world alive I awoke

In the winter of 1995, petitioned by Bob Dylan to tour with him along the east coast, we assembled the *Gone Again* crew. Lenny, Jay Dee, Tony, Oliver, and Tom Verlaine formed the band and friends and family were added for good measure. On the tour bus, Michael Stipe donated his expertise at the microwave, providing special nachos for us all.

This was a joyful period for me, of comradeship; of shaking off the performance dust. The highlight came from the opportunity to accompany Bob on a song of my choice. I chose "Dark Eyes." Singing with the one who had been an inspiration and influence on my work was an experience I shall always cherish.

Wing

I was a wing in heaven blue
Soared over the ocean
Soared over Spain
And I was free
Needed nobody
It was beautiful
It was beautiful

I was a pawn
Didn't have a move
Didn't have nowhere
That I could go
But I was free
I needed nobody
It was beautiful
It was beautiful

And if there's one thing
Could do for you
You'd be a wing
In heaven blue

I was a vision
In another eye
And they saw nothing
No future at all
Yet I was free
I needed nobody
It was beautiful
It was beautiful

And if there's one thing
Could do for you
You'd be a wing
In heaven blue

Ravens

Common fortune seeks us all
And slips our binding rings
We'll turn our heads
And make us reel
We'll bare our arms as wings

Before our feet a feather drifts
Beyond us it will fall
'Cause time will bid and make us rise
Make ravens of us all

My loved he breathed the air of kings
Yet fell beneath his luck
And in his heart a yearning yet
Before his time time shook
And all the gifts that god had gave
And those by fate denied
Gone to where all treasures laid
And where the raven flies

Oh there are places I agree
Where I have yet to roam
The Egyptian field the arctic sea
Where shadows haunt and moan
But none but sky I have to go
Should I return to thee
Gone to where the feather flies
To eternity
But for a time I got more time
Till I a raven be

'Cause time will bid
And make us rise
Make ravens of us all

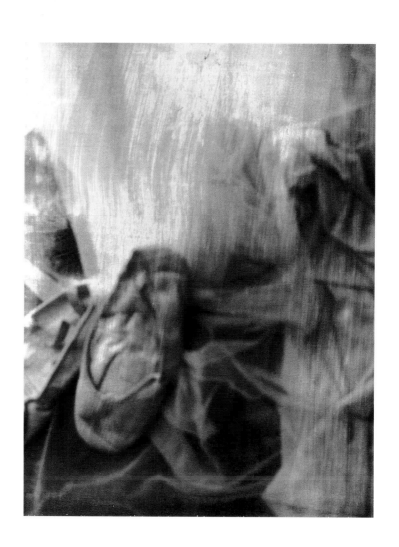

Fireflies

I been a'walking
Wherefore am I walking
I been a'walking
If you see me walking
A'walking a'wandering
If you see me walking
Don't ever turn your eye
Don't turn away don't turn away
I'm coming to you
Eleven steps till I can rest
Eleven steps till I'm blessed by you
I and I alone can but do for you
To twist in my hand the thorn of thy youth
To draw thy seed to turn in birth
Thy sighs thy moans I and I alone
Nine steps till I can rest
Nine steps till I'm blessed by you
I will wash your feet and dry them with my hair
I will give to you every other tear
Thy mouth thy spear thy season of mirth
Seven steps until I can rest
Seven steps till I'm blessed by you
All I ever wanted I wanted I wanted
All I ever wanted I wanted from you
Thy highs thy lows I and I alone
Ghost of thy ghost walk I will walk
A burning stem to illume thy night
Five steps till I can rest
Five steps till I'm blessed by you
Four steps until I can rest
Four steps till I'm blessed by you
Three steps until I get to you
Two steps until I can rest
Two steps till I'm blessed by you
Blood of my blood bone of my bone
Can but do for you I and I alone

Farewell Reel

It's been a hard time
And when it rains
It rains on me
The sky just opens
And when it rains
It pours

I walk alone
Assaulted it seems
By tears of heaven
And darling I can't help
Thinking those tears are yours

Our wild love came from above
And wilder still
Is the wind that howls
Like a voice that knows it's gone
'Cause darling you died
And well I cried
But I'll get by
Salute our love
And send you a smile
And move on

So darling farewell
All will be well
And then all will be fine
The children will rise
Strong and happy be sure
'Cause your love flows
And the corn still grows
And God only knows
We're only given
As much as the heart can endure

But I don't know why
But when it rains
It rains on me
The sky just opens
And when it rains
It pours

But I look up
And a rainbow appears
Like a smile from heaven
And darling I can't
Help thinking that smile
Is yours

Come Back Little Sheba

Come back little Sheba
I hear them calling
Open your eyes
Awake from thy sleep
High above
The stars are falling
Open your arms
And you shall receive

The lights of the city
So bold and flashing
All of its riches
Imparted to thee
Robes of saffron
Robes of standing
A road of crimson
Spread at your feet

Your robes of standing
Your robes of saffron
Your road of crimson
All pleasing to me
But close your lights
Close your gates
I must arise
My flock awaits

Farewell little Sheba
I hear them a'calling
Here is your staff
Tend to thy sheep
Good wishes be with you
If that be your calling
Farewell little Sheba
Arise and take leave

Peace and Noise

Through the empty arch comes a wind, a mental wind blowing relentlessly over the heads of the dead, in search of new landscapes and unknown accents...announcing the constant baptism of newly created things.

— Federico García Lorca, *In Search of Duende*

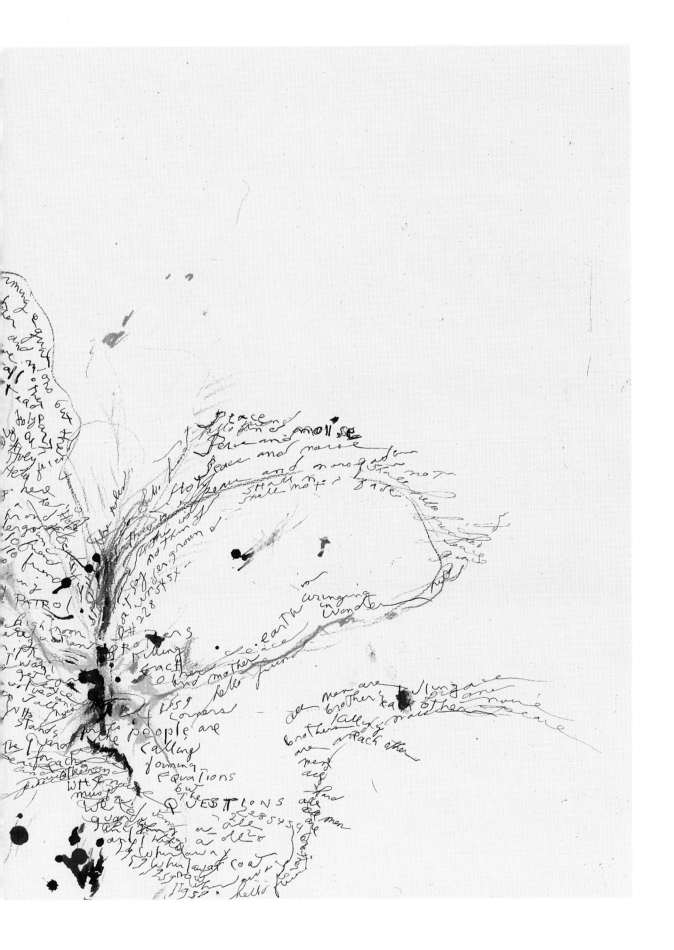

William Seward Burroughs

February 5, 1914 – August 2, 1997

GREETINGS. Labor Day approaches. Our labors near complete. Just perhaps the hope of uncovering one last thing, as I write, a few more words. But all words are covered save those wound about a spool and as those unwind, forming a prayer of their own, we repeat that which is taught by those that were taught before. And how can we tell if this teaching is true. By its own existence. For it is as formed from that which formed the word. And if it came to one, was it not sent? We consider this as we scrape the dying earth from the bottoms of our shoes. The sheriff is dead, long live the sheriff.

The dead speak, but we as a people have forgotten how to listen. We hold them in our hands, they course through our blood. They are found in the leaves of the Koran, the Psalms, the Torah, the Constitution, the New Testament. All revelations, all poetry, all the sacred books. They send words of love and woe. And we entwine their ideas with our own, forming a new body. Labor Day approaches. Let us now salute our neighbor. His trials both honorable and pathetic are our own. So we can laugh and also weep. The sheriff is dead, long live the sheriff.

Our neighbors await. The great conscience awaits and the pool of memory, distance and dream. The sheriff is dead. And did he not love us. Did he not magnify our spirit, our very gait by simply existing. And now, what is our task? The new century awaits and how shall we slouch toward it. What vows will we utter. What fruit shall we pluck from perspiring limbs. And who will be first and who will be last, and will we do the right thing or is there a right thing, or just simply existence formed and reformed by our labors gathering.

In early April, during the recording process of *Peace and Noise*, Allen Ginsberg passed away. Oliver Ray had composed "Spell," over which the band, comprised of Lenny Kaye, Jay Dee Daugherty, Tony Shanahan, Oliver, and myself, performed Allen's "Footnote to Howl."

William Burroughs died in early August, as we finished our work. Oliver and I flew to St. Louis to greet the funeral procession, winding from Lawrence, Kansas. All white. With William in the forefront in a white hearse. There we gathered in his name, offering a final salute before commending him to the earth. Thus saying farewell to Allen and William, the best minds of their generation.

Waiting Underground

If you believe all your hope is gone
Down the drain of your human kind
The time has arrived
You be waiting here
As I was in a snow white shroud
Waiting underground

There by the ridge
Be a gathering
Beneath the pilgrim moon
There we shall await
The beat of your feet
Hammering the earth
Where the great ones tremble
In their snow white shrouds
Waiting underground

If you seek the kingdom
Come, come along
Waiting by the ridge
There be a gathering
Beneath the pilgrim moon
Where the river thunders

Where we shall await,
The beat of your feet
Hammering the earth and as the earth resounds
Where the great ones tremble
And your human kind becomes as one
Then we will arise
In our snow white shrouds
We will be as one, but until that day
There we shall await
In our snow white shrouds
Waiting underground
In our snow white shrouds
Waiting underground

Whirl Away

Hello friend I've come a calling
Passively stationed active patrol
Sliding in high noon
Like some reluctant sheriff
Not want to get involved in it all
Who stands guard for each other
Why must we guard anything at all
Anything at all

From the earth's four corners the people are calling
Forming equations but the questions are hard
All men are brothers killing each other
And mother earth is wringing in wonder
Who stands guard for each other
Why must we guard anything at all. Anything at all
Whirl away now
Whirl away now
Whirl away now
Whirl away

There's a cross on the road, there's a great mill turning
Some seeking answers, some are born with answers
You can hold on the blade and turn around forever
Be flung into space into another kind of grace
Who stands guard for each other
Why must we guard anything at all. Anything at all
Whirl away now
Whirl away now
Whirl away now
Whirl away

Some give of the hand,
some give of their land
Some giveth their life
Lying in a field of grain the staff of life all around you
Yet you will cut someone down for their possessions

Some material thing
And our children are being blown away
Like wishes in the wind
For the sake of their coat
Or their colors or their code
Or the color of their skin
Or the name of their shoes
And the mother cries why'd they take my son
And the father wonders why'd they take my boy
He extended his hand he gave of his land
He gave of his bread he gave of his heart
Said hello friend
Hello friend
Hello friend
Hello friend

IN grammar school my classmates and I were wrenched from the wisdom of Uncle Wiggily and made to parade single-file into the depths of a makeshift fallout shelter. There we lay facedown among the stores of Spam, generic goods, and bottled water. It was peace, fifties fashion. Preparing for the bomb. Thus it was revealed our elders who had fought for our freedom had spent equal time inventing methods and self-annihilation.

As the decade rolled on, dressed in Davy Crockett gear, I clocked my world. *Life* magazine kept me posted. Picasso. Nazi war criminals. Jackson Pollock. Korea. The Beats. The death of Charlie Parker. The rise of Fidel Castro. By 1959, "Stagger Lee" was on the radio, *Naked Lunch* under the counter. Conformity was on the high rise. And cars looked just as ambitious.

As for me, I had turned in my coonskin cap and spent long hours in the library. I had discovered Tibet—the Dalai Lama, the great monasteries, and the prayer flags bracing the bright Himalayan wind. In March, while gathering material for a school paper, my Tibet was invaded by the Chinese. I was horrified to report the mass slaughter, imprisonment of monks and nuns, the burning of their temples, and the forced exile of their spiritual leader. At twelve years old I was unable to comprehend the public's disinterest. The general lack of outrage. Feeling helpless, I stood before my window at bedtime and said my prayers for the Dalai Lama and his people as wild-winged Chevrolets flew through the night.

1959

Listen to my story, got two tales to tell
One of fallen glory, one of vanity
The world's roof was raging
We were looking fine
Cause we built that thing
And it grew wings
In 1959

Wisdom was a teapot, pouring from above
Desolation angels served it up with love
Igniting life every form of light
Moved by bold design
Slid in that thing
And it grew wings
In 1959

It was blue and shining in the sun
Braced, native
Speeding the American plain
Into freedom freedom freedom

China was a tempest and madness overflowed
The lama was a young man and watched his world in flames
Taking glory down by the edge of clouds
It was a crying shame
Another lost horizon Tibet the fallen star
Wisdom and compassion crushed in the land of Shangri-la
But in the land of the Impala honey, well we were looking fine
Cause we built that thing and it grew wings in 1959
Cause we built that thing and it grew wings in 1959
Cause we built that thing and it grew wings in 1959

It was the best of times, it was the worst of times in 1959
It was the best of times, it was the worst of times in 1959

Don't Say Nothing

Lower the thing the skin of a cat
Skin it to the left just laying there
No other thing is luck like that
And you set it said it said nothing

Went to the party very discouraged
I watched the litter pile like a wall
I looked at the river just couldn't forgive it
It was ladened with all kinds of shit
Still I admit that I didn't say nothing
I turned my back walked away
Got to face the fact that I didn't say nothing

Everyone was dancing I stood over in the corner
I was listening they were saying this and saying that
And putting this one down but nothing was delivered
Nothing good was coming I just stood there
I couldn't believe it but I didn't say nothing
I walked the floor then I looked away
Got to face the fact that I didn't say nothing

How long how long will we make do
Maybe it's time to break on through
Gonna lift my skirts gonna straighten up
Gonna get well I'm gonna do something
Gonna face the fact gonna give it back
And I'm gonna do something won't hold my tongue
Won't hold the thought won't hold the card
Well I'm gonna do something
Oh my brain I got to complain
You can refrain but I'm gonna do something
How long how long will we make do
Maybe it's time to break on through

Out in the desert I saw that old cat skinned
I saw it floating in the river
I saw and no one seemed to mind
They sat there they sat there watching the sun
I saw it float away and I watched the buildings crumble
Like dust in the hand and we watched the sun
Spread its wings and fly away
And in the mountains a cry echoes
Don't say nothing
Don't say nothing no
Don't say nothing no

Dead City

This dead city longs to be
This dead city longs to be free
Seven screaming horses
Melt down in the sun
Building scenes on empty dreams
And smoking them one by one

This dead city longs to be
This dead city longs to be living
Is it any wonder there's squalor in the sun
With their broken schemes and their lotteries
They never get nowhere

Is it any wonder they're spitting at the sun
God's parasites in abandoned sites
And they never have much fun

If I was a blind man
Would you see for me
Or would you confuse
The nature of my blues
And refuse a hand to me

Is it any wonder crying in the sun
Is it any wonder I'm crying in the sun
Well I built my dreams on your empty scenes
Now I'm burning them one by one

This damn city this dead city
Immortal city
Motor city
Suc-cess city
Longs to be
Longs to be
Free
Free
Free

Blue Poles

Mother as I write the sun dissolves
Blood life streaming cross my hand
And these words, these words
Hope dashed immortal hope
Hope streaking the canvas sky
Blue poles infinitely winding, as I write, as I write
Blue poles infinitely winding, as I write, as I write

We joined the long caravan
Hungry dreaming going west
Just for work just to get a job
And we never got lucky
We just forged on
And the dust the endless dust
Like a plague it covered everything
Hal fell with the fever
And mother I did what I could
Blue poles infinitely winding, as I write, as I write
Blue poles infinitely winding, as I write, as I write

We prayed we prayed for rain
I never wanted to see the sun again

All my dresses you made by hand
We left behind on the road
Hal died in my arms
We buried him by the river
Blue poles infinitely winding, as I write, as I write
Blue poles infinitely winding, as I write, as I write

Death Singing

In the straw-colored light
In light rapidly changing
On a life rapidly fading

Have you seen death singing
Have you seen death singing

With a throat smooth as a lamb
Yet dry as a branch not snapping
He throws back his head
And he does not sing a thing mournful

Have you seen death singing
Have you seen death singing
Have you seen death singing
In the straw-colored light

He sings a black embrace
And white opals swimming
In a child's leather purse
Have you seen death swimming
Have you seen death swimming

With a throat smooth as a lamb
Yet dry as a branch not snapping
He throws back his head
And he does not sing a thing mournful

Have you seen death singing
Have you seen death singing
Have you seen death singing
In the straw-colored light

He sings of youth enraged
And the burning of Atlanta
And these viral times
And May ribbons streaming
And straw-colored curls a-turning
A mother's vain delight
And woe to the sun
And woe to the dawn
And woe to the young
Another hearse is drawn
Have you seen death singing
In the straw-colored light

Chapu: "JOAN OF ARC."

ALPHA

"Memento Mori" is pure improvisation, spun off a Bo Diddley beat. While recording, we broke free from "Not Fade Away" into a realm of our own. It was hot and humid, and we were spent. Still agitated, we went for another pass. It had been my intention to tell a story of the last hours of Blind Lemon Jefferson. Imagining him in the center of a storm, in a fine old greatcoat, bracing the Chicago wind, his heart giving out, and him falling like some heavy angel upon an expanse of pure snow with his spectacles lying beside him, looking up at the white flakes swirling like dancing children celebrating Blind Lemon seeing at last.

We were recording in a converted propeller factory and maybe it was the place or maybe the heat and the turn of the fans against the whirring of amplifiers, but I was put in mind of helicopter blades, and the Vietnam War, and those that fell, and the monument on the hill, and *Apocalypse Now*, and we just went that way. I grabbed ahold of one of those blades and it was all there mapped out.

Not just the war, not just the story of one soldier, but of all human existence; the simple knowledge that we all support the grand scheme with its demons and angels, its sacred bums, its laborers, the misbegotten, the revered, the lowest of the low. All contributing to the consciousness of the great whole—a magnificent flowering network unfolding without end in all directions.

Thus, the soldier blown from the sky, the mutilated runaway, the leper untouched, and the laundress unnoticed, those never searched for, those not enshrouded nor prayed for all possess a more radiant face within knowledge. For knowledge is its own body, the fluxiant body of mankind. It is the whole of human history. For as breath is known every man is known. Cradled in the hand of the mind. An infinite souvenir.

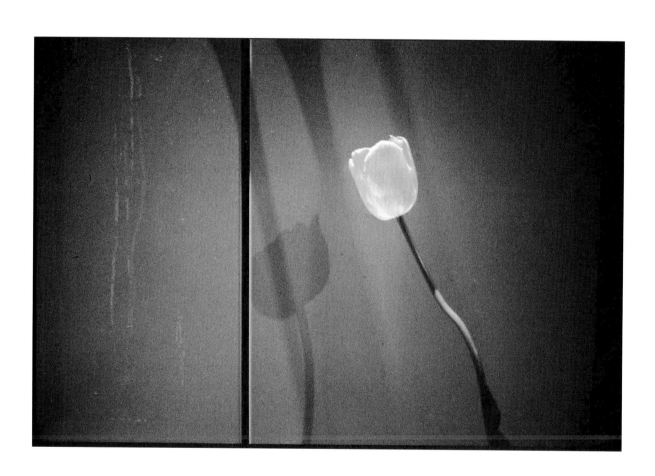

Memento Mori

The fan whirling like the blades of a copter
Lifting into the skies above a foreign land
Fire and iron soaked with the bodies of so many friends
Johnny waved. He was on his way home
He waved good-bye to his comrades in arms
And all the twisted things he had seen
He waved good-bye
And the blades hit something
Maybe just fate but the blades hit
The copter went up in flames
And Johnny never went marching home
And Johnny never went marching home
They took his name and they carved it on a slab of marble
With several thousand other names
All the fallen idols
The apples of their mother's eye
Just another name

Meanwhile back on the burning shore
Johnny's comrades stood speechless
They looked with misbelieving eyes
Cause there were bits of metal and the embers
The embers of his eyes fanned out in the air
Black dust flames. Oh Johnny
Someday they'll make a movie about you
And in the making of that movie, some mad apocalypse
It will become even stranger than the simple act
Just a boy going up. Up. Up
Just a boy going up. Up. Up

In flames the smoke
Just another life
Just another breath
And who'll remember
Oh eternity now
As eternal as a sheet of marble
Eternal as a slab

On a green hill
And your name
And all your fallen brothers
And all the ones not cut
All the ones remembered
Only in the hearts
A mother a father a brother
A sister a lover son daughter
Young man shall not fade shall not fade
Your ancestors salute you greet you
And the gods of your ancestors salute you
Having been formed by the mind of your ancestors
The gods of your ancestors salute you
Having been formed by your ancestors
The gods of your ancestors salute you
They draw you in
They draw you through
They draw they draw you
Through that golden door
Come on in boy
We remember you
We conceived you
We conceived of your breath
We conceived of the whole human race
And we conceived it to be a beautiful thing
Like a tulip bending in the wind
Sometimes it comes back to us
In the form of the hand filled with dust
Comes back in the form of a smitten child
Our raped daughters
The broken bones
Souls cleaved of hearts
They come back to us

Our hands are filled
With their rotting tissues
But we turn not our backs
We press our lips
Into their cancer
Into the dust
Into the remains of each one
And that love is there
And will greet you
Come on in boy
It's eternal love

Well here go ahead
Run through that plane
Oh man running through your mind
You took a cat
You took a life
You took it by the tail
And you swirled it around your head
And you thrashed it
You smashed the life out of it
Then you knew that would be your own
But you wanted to feel the dying
Because you knew
You would feel your own
You would feel your own
But you're remembered
You're remembered
You're remembered good
We remember
We remember
We remember
Everything

EASTER arrived late in 1997. *Peace and Noise* near complete we took a holiday in Provincetown. We camped in a modest spot by the sea. It was my hope to lay work aside, to do nothing but dutifully love life and to contemplate the events in human history that led to the crucifixion and to Christ revealing, at great cost, the process of his transfiguration. An act one can barely comprehend in these scientific times.

These things ran through my mind when the news flashed that thirty-nine people were found dead by their own hand or by the hand of a comrade. The suicides of Heaven's Gate. And what their leader did and what they did deeply disturbed me. Thus Easter was not spent as I had imagined. But in a small room with the windows overlooking the street and the venetian blinds barely slatted.

Oliver and I worked through the evening into the night and wrote "Last Call." When we returned to the studio, the band recorded it, Michael Stipe joining us on the refrain.

It is our response to the mass suicide. Our hope being it will remind one to think for himself and above all value and respect one's life on earth. For life is the best thing we have in this existence. And if we should desire to believe in something, it should be a beacon within. This beacon being the sun, sea, and sky, our children, our work, our companions and, most simply put, the embodiment of love.

Last Call

In a mansion high the young man stood
Ready to join his companions good
Outside the scent of magnolia blossoms
Down streets of gold the children were racing

Just another wandering soul
Adrift among the stars
Just another human heart
Led, led away

He put his shoes on and he laid down
Outside the clouds were swiftly gathering
He drained his cup and he stirred the mixture
And he closed his eyes as his conscience whispered

Just another wandering soul
Adrift among the stars
Just another human heart
Led, led away

Misgivings unspoken he joined his companions
His face covered over in a mansion high
Outside the children gazed in wonder
At the quickening sky then slowly disbanded

Thirty-nine wandering souls
Adrift among the stars
Thirty-nine human hearts
Led, led away

His burning skin cooled by angels
Swallowing sorrows excretion
It's all excretion
Felled by his hand or the mind of another man
Who makes the decisions
Lends no provisions for mere eternal rides
Learning of course every alien force

Even Christ yearns to be
To possess the skin
And bone the blood of man
Who tends the flock who breaks the bread
Who makes his own choices
Won't listen to voices
Accept no false teachers
False preachers, good deeders
With their hands out stretched
To be filled with your money
Your mind, your heart, your imagination
Sympathy, empathy
Acknowledge all man as fellow creation
But don't follow him
Don't be led away

Notes for the Future

august 2, 1998, new york city

What did we want
What did we ever want
To shake the fragile hands of time
To rip from their sockets
Deceiving eyes
To ride through the night
In a three cornered hat
Against the shadows
To cry Awake Awake
Wake up arms delicate feet
We are paramount then obsolete
Wake up throat wake up limbs
Our mantle pressed
from palm to palm
Wake up hearts dressed in rags
Costly garments fall away
Dangle now in truthful threads
That bind the breast
And wind the muscle
Of the soul and whole together

Listen my children and you shall hear
The sound of your own steps
The sound of your hereafter
Memory awaits and turns to greet you
Draping its banner across your wrists
Wake up arms delicate feet
For as one to march the streets
Each alone each part of another
Your steps shall ring
Shall raise the cloud
And they that will hear will hear
Voice of the one and the one and the one
As it has never been uttered before
For something greater yet to come
Than the hour of the prophets
In their great cities
For the people of Ninevah
Fell to their knees
Heeding the cry of Jonah
United covering themselves in sackcloth
And ashes and called to their God
And all their hearts were as one heart
And all their voices were as one voice
God heard them and his mind was moved
Yet something greater will come to pass
And who will call and what will they call
Will they call to God the air the fowl
It will not matter if the call is true
They shall call and this is known
One voice and each another
Shall enter the dead
The living flower
Enter forms that we know not
To be felt by sea by air by earth
And shall be an elemental pledge
This our birthright
This our charge
We have given over to others
And they have not done well
And the forests mourn the leaves fall
Swaddling babes watch and wonder
As the fathers of our spirit nations
Dance in the streets in celebration

As the mountains turn pale
From their nuclear hand
And they have not done well
Now my children
You must overturn the tables
Deliver the future from material rule
For the only rule to be considered
Is the eleventh commandment
To love one another
And this is our covenant
Across your wrist
This offering is yours
To adore adorn
To bury to burn
Upon a mound
To hail
To set away
It is merely a cloth merely our colors
Invested with the blood of a people
All their hopes and dreams
It has its excellence yet it is nothing
It shall not be a tyranny above us
Nor should God nor love nor nature
Yet we hold as our pleasure
This tender honor
That we acknowledge the individual
And the common ground formed
And if our cloth be raised and lowered
Half mast what does this tell us
An individual has passed
Saluted and mourned by his countrymen
This ritual extends to us all
For we are all the individual
No unknown no insignificant one
Nor insignificant labor nor act of charity
Each has a story to be told and retold
Which shall be as a glowing thread
In the fabric of man
And the children shall march
And bring the colors forward
Investing within them
The redeeming blood
Of their revolutionary hearts

Let it come. Let it come.
The time we dream of.

> —Arthur Rimbaud,
> "Song of the Highest Tower"

Tₕₑ author wishes to thank the following, who contributed their photographs for inclusion in this book, in order of appearance:

Oliver Ray: Typewriter/pg. v; Rimbaud in frame/pg. vi; Untitled/pg. 194; *Peace and Noise*/pg. 197; Tulip/pg. 224; Rosary/pg. 231; Untitled/pg. 233; Bound Flag/pg. 233. Avedon's studio/pg. 241; Bound Flag ii/pg. 248.

Linda Bianucci: Hoedown Hall/pg. viii; With Kimberly/pg. 20

Judy Linn: Wall, 23rd Street, NYC, 1971/pgs. x-xi; With Dylan mask, 1971/ pg. 1; Outtake *Radio Ethiopia*/pg. 43

Eve Arnold: Lotte Lenya (reprinted by permission Magnum Photos)/pg. xii

Robert Mapplethorpe: Rooftop, Chelsea Hotel, 1970/pg. xiii; *Horses*/pg. 3; Outtake *Horses,* 1975/pg. 4; Cross, 1984/pg. 71; Still Moving, 1978/pg. 72; Still Moving, 1978/pg. 73; With Rickenbacker, 1978/pg. 74; Still Moving, 1978/pg. 83; Outtake *Wave*, 1979/pg. 105; Family, 1979/pg. 129; *Dream of Life,* 1987/pg. 131; Smith family, 1987/pg. 133; "People Have the Power," 1986/pg. 134; Sam Wagstaff, 1978/pg. 140; With butterfly, 1987/pg. 145; Waves, 1980/pg. 149; Self-portrait, 1982/pg. 157; American Flag, 1977/pg. 161

David Gahr: Todd Smith (© David Gahr)/pg. xvii

Kate Simon: Richard Sohl/pg. 14; Hobby horse, Boston, 1977/pg.19; With William Burroughs, Franklin Street, NYC/pg. 28; PSG at CBGB, 1975/pg. 36; December 30, 1975/pg. 39; Men's room, Hofstra University/pg. 48; Taco Rico, NYC/pg. 56; Physical therapy, NYC/pg. 69; Richard Sohl at Carl Apfelschnitt's printing studio, NYC, 1977/pg. 79; With clarinet, NYC, 1978/pg. 114; Richard Sohl, NYC, 1984/pg. 158; William Burroughs, Lawrence, Kansas, 1987/pg. 200

Bill Yoscary: With Allen Ginsberg, Gotham Book Mart, NYC/pg. 27

Godlis: CBGB, 4 A.M./pg. 29; Television, CBGB, 1976/pg. 37; Neck brace, CBGB, 1977/pgs. 60-61; Manhole, NYC/pg. 63; Final show, Palladium, NYC, 1979/pg. 127; Hoboken Awareness Day, Hoboken, NJ, 1997/pgs. 210-11; With clarinet, CBGB, Halloween, 1997/pg. 217; Jackson, Hoboken, 1997/pg. 234 (© Photos by Godlis)

Bart Everly: Horse/pg. 30

Cynthia Black: PSG, Locker room; pgs. 33-35

Linda McCartney: Jimi Hendrix (reprinted with grateful acknowledgment to the Linda McCartney Foundation)/pg. 40

Donna Santisi: With Fender Duo-Sonic/pg. 47; Red Rocks, Colorado, 1997/pg. 205

Jenny Stern: Backbend, 1976/pg. 51; With Fender Duo-sonic, 1977/pg. 64

Jody Caravaglia: r.e.f.m./pg. 53; Patti Smith Group, 1978/pg. 120-21

Frank Stefanko: Richard Sohl, NYC/pg. 55

Annie Liebovitz: Boots/pg. 77; Cains/pg. 84; Live performance, 1978/pg. 88; PSG live, 1978/pgs. 90-91; Airport/pg. 93; Hotel/pg. 94; Live performance/ pg. 101; Arlington Cemetery/pgs. 106, 109; Cains/pg. 110; Ivan Kral/pg. 113; Lincoln Memorial/pg. 117; With Todd/pg. 119; Suitcase/pg. 126; *Gone Again,* 1996/pg. 163; With Jesse, 1996/pg. 186

Lynn Goldsmith: Single sleeve for "Because the Night," 1978. (© 1978, Arista Records, Inc.)/pg. 80

Robert Matheu: Masonic Temple, Detroit, 1977/pg. 97; Second Chance, Ann Arbor, 1979/pg. 99

Wyatt Troll: Music stand, Electric Lady Studios, NYC/pg. 165

Steven Sebring: Acoustic guitar and Fender Twin, Michigan/pg. 169; Stairwell, Michigan/pg. 174; Lenny Kaye, London, 1997/pg. 176; London, 1997/pg. 179; London, 1997/pgs. 180-81; Stairwell, Chelsea Hotel/pg. 182

Andy Glass and Barry Cawston: Oliver Ray/pg. 171

Kevin Mazur: Kurt Cobain/pg. 172; With Bob Dylan, Orpheum (courtesy of Kevin Mazur)/pg. 185

Michael Stipe: Marquis, Boston/pg. 184; Jay Dee Daugherty/pg. 213

Jem Cohen: Central Park Near the Good Tree, 1997/pg. 202; Tibetan bowl, Prague, 1996/pg. 206; CBGB, Halloween, 1997/pg. 214; Yik Wong and Tony Shanahan/pg. 216; Oliver Ray/pg. 216; Foot pedals/pg. 217; Kafka's grave/ pg. 228; Endpapers, CBGB

Michael Ackerman: Benjamin, 1997/pg. 221

Patti Hudson: Jesse, Detroit, 1995/pg. 239

Archival Sources and Private Collections

Johnny Carson, 1955. (Corbis=Bettmann)/pg. ix

Maria Callas (Corbis=Bettmann)/pg. xx

John Coltrane (Michael Ochs Archives, Venice, CA)/pg. 13

Jean Genet at sixteen, 1927 (courtesy of Albert Dichy/Institut Mémoires de L'Édition Contemporaine)/pg. 86

Pope John Paul I (AP/World Wide Photos)/pg. 122

Endless Column, 1937. Constantin Brancusi (©1998 Artists Rights Society (ARS), New York/ADAGP, Paris)/pg. 189

Peace and Noise #1, mixed media on paper, Patti Smith (collection of Robin and Stuart Ray, Houston, Texas)/pgs. 198-99

Jackson Pollock and Lee Krasner, 1950. Hans Namuth (courtesy of the Hans Namuth Foundation)/pg. 218

Personal Archives: Manuscript, piss factory/pg. vii; Format, first poetry reading/pg. x; Age six/pg. xviii; "Vera Gemini," first song/pg. xxii; Single sleeve, "Gloria," photo by Paul Kasko, *Photorock*/pg. 6; B-side/p. 7; Notes for "Redondo Beach"/pg. 10; Photo booth, Linda/pg. 10; Todd, bootcamp/pg. 23; Map, Pere Lachaise, Jim Morrison grave site, 1973/pg. 24; Graffiti across from Morrison's grave, Paris/pgs. 26-27; Fragment, 1971/pg. 26; Flier, 1977/pg. 45; Rat/Art, 1977/pg. 52; Field Marshall/pg. 53; Rock n Roll Nigger Manifesto/pg. 87; Genet obituary/pgs. 86-87; Postcard/pg. 102; Young Richard Sohl at piano, photograph by Mike Elliott/pg.123; *Wave* flier/pg.124; Beverly and Grant Smith, Upper Darby, PA, 1946/pg. 137; French Guyana/pg. 153; Sleeping, 1985/pg. 154; Visa photo by Dr. Lam/pg. 159; Fred, Michigan/pg. 166; Nureyev's slippers/pg. 190; Acoustic guitar/pg. 193; Dalai Lama (courtesy of Tibet Image Bank)/pg. 208; Joan of Arc postcard, from Robert/pg. 222

245

Index to Songs

THE author gratefully acknowledges the Estate of Robert Mapplethorpe, Annie Liebovitz, and the Liebovitz studio for their generous support.

The lyrics in this book are the result of nearly three decades of collaboration. With the exception of a handful of my own songs, all of the music has been written or cowritten by these musicians: Lenny Kaye, Ivan Kral, Richard Sohl, Jay Dee Daugherty, Allen Lanier, Tom Verlaine, Fred Sonic Smith, Oliver Ray, and Tony Shanahan.

My appreciation to Rosemary Carroll and to my editor, Betsy Lerner.

Special thanks to Brian Mulligan, Nancy Henderson, Andi Ostrowe, Michael Stipe, Andreas Brown, Patti Hudson, Jessie Zoldak, Lisa Robinson, Clive Davis, and Arista Records.

PUBLISHED BY DOUBLEDAY

a division of Bantam Doubleday Dell Publishing Group, Inc.
1540 Broadway, New York, New York 10036

DOUBLEDAY and the portrayal of an anchor with a dolphin
are trademarks of Doubleday, a division of
Bantam Doubleday Dell Publishing Group, Inc.

BOOK DESIGN BY BRIAN MULLIGAN

Every reasonable effort has been made to trace the ownership of all
copyrighted photographs included in this volume. Any errors which
may have occurred are inadvertent and will be corrected in subsequent
editions, provided notification is sent to the publisher.

Library of Congress Cataloging-in-Publication Data
Smith, Patti.
[Songs, Texts]
Patti Smith complete: lyrics, reflections, and notes for the future.
  p.   cm.
1. Rock music—Texts.   I. Title
ML54.6.S64P38   1998 <case>
782.42166'0268--dc2   98-23417
        CIP   MN

0-385-49079-8

Printed in the United States of America

November 1998

First Edition